# How to Fearlessly and Successfully Ask for Money

# How to Fearlessly and Successfully Ask for Money

Mike G. Williams

How to Fearlessly and Successfully Ask for Money
by Mike G. Williams

Published by CreateSpace Independent Publishing
Platform

ISBN: 978-1543014518
Copyright © 2017 by Mike G. Williams
Cover design by Adam Hall, atomcreative.net

For more information on the author, visit:
www.FocusOnTheBanquet.com

Library of Congress Cataloging-in-Publication Data
Williams, Mike G.
How to Fearlessly and Successfully Ask for Money /
Mike G. Williams, 1st ed.

Printed in the United States of America

# CHAPTER SUMMARIES / TABLE OF CONTENTS

## PREFACE – Who should read this book?

## INTRODUCTION / The God Factor Plus You

Do you believe that God believes in your ministry? Could your financial records prove that in a court of law? God is a team player. God works in tandem with the effort of His children, and when God is working, there is nobody you would rather have on your team. He matches the labor of His children. He rewards those who will work with wisdom, determination, and sacrifice. Successful fundraising may not be easy, but the results of a wise, well-planned presentation is rewarded supernaturally when the infusion of God happens.

## Chapter 1 / What Every Great Donor Needs

There are seven needs every donor requires from your organization:

1. Need a clear understanding of the situation or problem.
2. Need to be inspired to be part or all of the solution.
3. Need a clear, unwavering cost of that solution.
4. Need confidence in your organization to complete the task.
5. Need to be personally asked to meet that need.
6. Need to be thanked thoroughly and properly.
7. Need to be given proof the project was successfully completed.

You will not bring new donors to your table or inspire previous donors to give you more until you meet their donor needs.

## Chapter 2 / Start a Millionaires Club

You must bring your donors into the inner sanctum of trust and friendship through relationship. Upon doing so, they will become lifetime donors. You must connect with your donors beyond your yearly banquet event. Find ways to bring new people to your doors while bringing fellowship to your stable donors.

## Chapter 3 / You Have Eight Seconds ... GO.    29

By the time many presenters reach the end of their first sentence, their listeners have reached the end of their ability to focus. A story that can be told quickly can be heard quickly, can be understood more clearly, and can be responded to more easily. Never edit a long story. Start with a short story and add only what is needed to move people. Remove anything from a story that doesn't drive your end purpose. You can tell any story in five sentences when you start with the end in mind.

## Chapter 4 / But I'm Not a Salesperson    61

Every great fundraising person is a great salesperson. There is nothing wrong with pushing a product, a theology, or a financial request, as long as what we are selling is genuinely good, honest, and upright. Wear your fundraiser badge as a badge of honor. You can learn the fine and meticulous art of fundraising.

## Chapter 5 / Twenty-five — One = Success    67

Fundraising can come with a large dose of rejection. Get over it. Keep track of your time between good connections and begin to see that time as the distance between two donations. Cover each mile with an attitude that says, "Only twenty-five miles to go." Accept each rejection as a milestone of joy, knowing that you are now one less call, visit, or dinner away from another great success.

## Chapter 6 / Carpe Diem    73

You cannot wait for the donor to approach you anymore than you can wait for a fully cooked fish to jump onto your plate. The successful fundraiser has a list of people they are actively pursuing a connection with. The successful fundraiser has a list of current donors and connects with them regularly. The successful fundraiser schedules "un-shakable / un- breakable" time slots each week to do nothing but work their specific list.

Apathetic fundraising techniques are just as ungodly as those who refuse to support your work. It's our job to cultivate every aspect of the donor relationship, not the donor's job to cultivate the relationship.

Streamline your giving process to make the actual exchange of money as easy and encouraging as your pitch. Those who aren't set up to receive the funds will see portions of their funding disappear before they can count it in the bank.

organizations are using to fund their ten- to fifty-year ministry plans.

## Chapter 18 / Eve ... And Adam                 167

Connecting with the married couple, as a team, is a key to higher donations. As a PRC, the women are already on your side. They get it, they love it, they see the need. We must not only equip women to bring their husbands to our events, we must have them present in our individual presentations. Sell the men. Sell the men. SELL THE MEN. Then you will go home successful.

## Chapter 19 / Finding Millennial Money        175

Drag your Millennials into a success story without getting political. Millennials see themselves as "world" people. Stay out of politics, and don't let any politics into your events, including political speakers. Don't offend, save lives. Decide what your message is. If your message is "Become Anti-Abortion Pro-Life," then work on that. But if your message is "Join us in rescuing babies and families," then make that your one and only message. Promote stories of total family success and its impact on the local or world community.

## Chapter 20 / Your Own Money Tree             185

Your organization needs an independent development account at your bank. They need to fund it with the gifts from your "inner circle" of board members, staff, and the super donors who understand that it takes money to make money. Use this account to fund all your fundraising efforts. Work wise. Work with business wisdom. Allow 100 percent of your donors' gifts to go to the project you are selling without having to take a penny to pay for their dinner lure. In the secular non-profit sectors, 100 percent to the project is rapidly becoming the new normal.

## Chapter 21 / One Effective Annual Ask        189

Most centers do a yearly fundraising banquet (now often called stewardship events). Bring your acquired knowledge of asking for money into every aspect of that event. Don't check your wisdom at the door—bring it in, let it roam about, let it bring you increased donations through wise financial communications. What you do in small groups does translate to larger groups.

## Chapter 22 / Deserve Good Funding

If we are going to ask for money with any degree of conscience, we need to make sure we're asking genuinely. Do we believe in our work? Does our work justify the money we are asking for to run it? Does our cost compare to other centers who are taking care of the same amount of clients? Is our board working or sitting? When we know that our product is good, we can sell it to anyone.

## Chapter 23 / Let's Remember Together

Those who cannot remember the past are forced to repeat it. Use this guide to prepare for your next presentation, which should be tomorrow. Use this guide to teach this material to someone in your office, for you never really know something until you teach it. The simplicity of this list will make it easy for you to incorporate the material into your everyday conversations and turn these conversations into increased dollars for your work.

## FOR YOUR INFORMATION

# PREFACE

## Who should read this book?

Are you and your board currently working at a level of financial effectiveness that fully funds your mission statement to overflowing? Is everyone on your team playing at a high level? Every staff member, board member, and everyone who has anything to do with the fundraising operations of a PRC or parachurch ministry should read this book. You either take a salary or have taken an oath of responsibility to help fund the ministry. This book will give you the ability to respond.

**Executive Directors** who need to present their organizations' work to the public with the expectation that generous funding will result from their presentation.

**Development Directors** charged with the responsibility of finding the funding to fully support their organization.

**Board Members** who take seriously their responsibility to fund the vision of the organization.

**Any person** who helps in raising money for their PRC or parachurch cause.

**Any person** who desires to make a passionate financial appeal for any cause will find the teaching in this manual effect changing.

**Any public speaker** who desires to move people in a way that demands action or active response from those people.

# INTRODUCTION

## The God Factor Plus You

**If any person lacks wisdom let him ask of God who gives to everyone and holds back nothing. — James 1:5**

Have you ever watched the wildly successful television show Shark Tank? Entrepreneurs seeking a large-dollar investment and personal involvement in their work stand before five billionaires. These entrepreneurs make their best presentation—often with tears—and then the Shark frenzy begins as these bleached, white-toothed human predators either fund their vision or rip them to shreds with insults. Why do some presenters succeed with seemingly mediocre inventions while others get chewed up while presenting brilliant ideas?

Most likely you're reading this book because you're an executive director who needs to help your center thrive, a development director who wants to be more successful, or a board member who wants to serve your PRC to a higher degree. This book will be profitable for any leader in any nonprofit who desires to learn to be extremely effective in asking for money.

**Large group events bring small and medium-sized gifts, but the person who knows how to make phenomenal one-to-one presentations will see the supersize sponsorships.**
**— Jack Eason**

Does your organization need a few supersize financial partners? In the following pages, I will equip you to make phenomenally successful fundraising presentations with confidence and comfort. I wlll share with you very honestly. You hold in your hand the wisdom I have learned in twenty-five years of standing before people and asking for money. Some of the material you may disagree with. I'm okay with that too. I disagreed with some of the material in this book at one time or another. I promise that this book will be financially worth the time you invest in reading it. Though this book is written with examples for the Pregnancy Resource Center movement, the principles apply to any parachurch organization.

**It always seems impossible, until it's done.**
**— Nelson Mandela**

Let's consider this scenario: You just stepped into an elevator and hit the button for floor twenty-two. The man already in the elevator is a well-known businessman. He looks at you and says, "I have ten thousand dollars in my left pocket. Before we get to the twenty-second floor, convince me that you need it more than the person I am going to meet." You have approximately ninety seconds. Can you do it? Do you know exactly what to say? Would your first words be "Uuuhhh…"? Every day, similar scenarios go past us, though rarely so blatantly. They are disguised in alternative premises and questions, but they are really asking to be told why you are the best place to put their charitable giving. People are looking for a place to make a mark of significance. When you believe that, you will see every introduction as an opportunity to help your mission while helping someone else fulfill their inner, more eternal need.

**When faced with a decision, many people say they are waiting for God. But we must understand that in most cases God is waiting for us.**
**— Andy Andrews**

I have asked that elevator-type scenario question to forty different non-profit directors in the last few weeks. Minutes before I took the platform to raise money for them, I simply said to each of them, "Help me speak to your audience tonight. I have ten thousand dollars in my pocket. In less than ninety seconds, tell me why you should get the money and not some competing charity." Thirty-eight of them explained that they would have to get back to me or think about it a while. Some launched sheepishly into how much it cost to do a ministry—not anything near what the question actually asked. The two who were able to articulate their response, answering many or most of the Seven Donor Needs, saw banner fundraising events. Not because they told me what to say, but because their entire event was driven by their knowledge of what it takes to move people to join their work. This book is going to teach you how to present your work in a way that answers the real questions donors have about your work.

This book was not titled Fundraising for Dummies or An Idiot's Guide to Raising Money for a reason. Idiots and dummies can't do a good job fundraising and won't do a good job fundraising. If you really believe you fall into that category, close the book. In fact, if you fall into that category, have the personal ethics to quit being involved in the leadership of any organization. That said, if you have the ability to think and learn, this book will transform your fundraising prowess and earn your organization great financial rewards. I will also promise wisdom in the fundraising arena will be delivered from God when we ask for it. We, in response, must be ready to take the wisdom and run with it.

Have you ever played tennis? I have. Well, many times I stood across from a professional while wearing white shorts on a green court. The pro knew how to play tennis. He served it to where he wanted, and I struggled to get it back over the net. My wimpish return came back to me rather rapidly and to the area of the court least near me. I ran with all my might, barely reaching it in time to awkwardly backhand it over the net. He then decidedly and strategically returned the ball to the farthest point from me … again. I ran. I tripped. I missed the ball. I bloodied my knees. This scenario was repeated until I was thoroughly beaten and somewhat convinced that God didn't really like me. I'm sure any onlookers felt sorry for me, and I'm sure that some laughed at my folly. I needed to learn to play tennis if I was going to compete at a higher level.

This is what I often see among my dear charitable organization friends. They have good energy. The have good intentions. They have great hearts. However, they lack the knowledge of how to do successful fundraising. In this book, I intend to change all that. In this book, I intend to teach you beyond the basics. I intend to teach you the foundations and the steps (not tricks) used by the seasoned professionals. This is not a book of tricks. This is not a book of secrets. This material is what every successful fundraiser knows already, and I am simply going to share that with you.

When I entered the fundraising court, I was like many of you—rather green behind the ears. Nevertheless, I was very fortunate to have been taken under the wing of some very, very successful men and women who really knew what they were doing. I was mentored by some genuine professionals who took me to school with the condition that I would, as one of them put it, "Shut up and listen," without questioning everything. I remember the day I asked a very well-known professional to be my mentor, thinking that he would jump at the chance to spend time on educating this amazing new hot shot (me). His response was a little less than enthusiastic. "Mike, I am sick of pouring my life into people only to have them ignore what I have spent blood, sweat, and tears to learn. I'm too old to waste my time anymore." I was somehow able to convince him that I would be willing to shut up and listen and do what he told me to do. I stopped long enough to listen and learn. As a result, I can boast some pretty amazing stats, much of those in direct response to this man's tutelage.

I am still learning. I hope to do that every day until they dig me a hole in the ground. That learning has allowed me to help organizations raise millions of dollars for very worthy causes. That learning has, as of the printing of this book, allowed me to be the most repeatedly booked fundraising speaker and among the highest money-raising PRC speakers in the entire United States for the past ten years. For the record, I intend to hold that position for at least another ten years.

You have this book in your hands because you want to bring your organization to a new financial level. Great. It will help you do that. This book has been written with specific information for my PRC, LIFE, and Adoption organizational friends, but its foundations and applications will benefit any charitable organization director who reads it with ears to hear.

### I wish I didn't know what I didn't know then. — Bob Seger

Unfortunately, many executive directors accepted their current position when the board hired them because of their passion for the cause, when in truth the board hired them subliminally believing they were somehow, because of that ministry passion, also going to be the big bread winner, the money tree, or the grand steam shovel of complete funding. Now both the board and the executive director are disappointed. It was not the executive director's fault the board didn't hire what they were really wanting. One observant trainer once said, "Most boards would do better to hire a development director or fundraising specialist first, and then bring on the staff that would be undergirded by the funding already in place." Nevertheless, it is what it is. Let's just move on from here and learn how to raise the money we need to do more than keep our doors open. Let's become what is needed.

**Failure doesn't mean you are a failure ...
it just means you haven't succeeded yet.
— Rev. Robert Schuller**

"Our community is in a slump." "Our oil and gas wells are down this year." "Nobody cares about this issue anymore." Don't buy the negativity lines. Those are excuses. You can succeed. You can prosper. There are plenty of organizations whose budget is being exceeded. You can be one of them.

"Brother Williams, we believe it's all in God's hands. We just need to pray more." Really? First, if you really believe that, are you fervently praying? Is your board fasting for your organization every week? Do you have a 24-hour prayer team going 365 days a year? If prayer is the only key, should we stop having a banquet and just pray? Ironically, the statistics show that God seems to bless those who are systematically making excellent fundraising presentations more than those who are not. I have often heard, "We just let God bring us the funds that He wants to bring us." After a decade and a half of doing this, I can tell you that God blesses the ones who do the best job of answering the donors' questions, meet the donors' needs, ask well for the money, and pray for the event. Some charities earn more than others, and wise leadership will learn from those charities. You do your part wisely and well, and God will mysteriously show up and bless your part to a greater degree.

**Stop pointing out problems.**
**Become part of the solution.**
**— Mark Batterson, Chasing the Lion**

Recently, a board member approached me at the end of a large, group fundraising presentation, one of around ninety I do each year. "Mr. Williams, all we need to do is pray more and more money will come in." With the adrenaline running high after a presentation, I responded a little more honestly than I should have. "Then any lack of funding is actually your fault. You didn't pray hard enough, long enough, and with enough fervency. Did you fast at all this week for unborn children and your PRC? Listen, my dear brother, if God is giving away eternal life with one simple prayer, why would He not fund our life-saving program with one simple prayer too, if prayer was all we needed to do?"

God works in tandem with people who pray and then wisely do what is needed to see victory. Think about my response more broadly before you toss my assertion aside as the ramblings of an over-theologically educated speaker. The greatest theological minds of our generation have prayed for years to end abortion, and it hasn't happened yet. If Billy Graham, Chuck Swindoll, Charles Stanley, and Max Lucado are not righteous enough to get this prayer answered, who is? My only deduction is to think that God must want us to have a part in the daily battle, not just the prayer team.

**Don't let prayer be an excuse for personal mediocrity.**
**— Paul Aldrich**

I will keep this teaching simple - simple - simple. There will be no pie charts, no projection analysis tables, and only one acronym. I'm going to help you succeed as a professional fundraiser by helping you think like a professional fundraiser and to think like a donor. The essays and material contained in this book will help you increase financially via whatever type of fundraiser you're producing. It will help you develop new revenue streams. As the old television show started, "Your mission, if you choose to accept it," is going to make you more money, more often.

**An athlete does not enjoy the pain of training; an athlete enjoys the results of having trained. — Andy Andrews**

As we talk about fundraising success, I am fully believing and expecting that the funds that I will so fervently equip you to raise will be used for an altruistic life-saving cause. If I wanted to simply train money makers, I would do an infomercial. Our financial windfall is not our end, but rather our beginning, as we exchange this money for the staff, goods, or services needed to save the lives of children and adults around the world.

Start the timer now. Don't let the Facebook, Instant Message, SnapChat, and whatever else distract you today. The cute cat videos will be there long after the money is gone. Tell the receptionist you can't be disturbed for anything shy of a hurricane for the next ninety minutes. Start by asking God (prayer) to use this book to deliver wisdom. Then read this book with a highlighter in your hand and a pen and paper by your side. Together, in partnership with

God, we will change your organization's financial future.

**If we do our bump and set properly,
we can count on God to spike the ball.
— Liz McCullough**

## TAKEAWAY:

In tandem with a wise and rather systematic God, we partner to bring the most amount of resources to our charity. Our partnership means that He brings His best and we bring our best to the table. We then expect the donor to return their best. Anything less than hard work and hard prayer will deliver you half of your potential.

## IMPERATIVE ASSIGNMENT:

This assignment is mandatory for you to track your own progress in your presentation skills. Please take out your smart phone and turn on the voice recorder. Imagine a wealthy philanthropist just met you in an elevator and requested to hear about your mission. He has ten thousand dollars in his pocket and has two minutes before your shared elevator lets him off at his stop. Don't preplan it. Don't rehearse. Record right now. Ready … set … go. If you don't have a recorder, write or type as much as you can in four minutes without editing. Scribble, write, type, or record now.

I promise that making this recording (or written record) will make all the difference in the outcome of your learning. Not doing it is saying you don't want the full benefit of this knowledge for your ministry. Yes, it is your choice. Think about this the next time those around you choose to do your assignment another way or not at all.

# 1

## What Every Generous Donor Needs

**Clearly, you are a letter from Christ showing the result of our ministry among you. It is carved not on tablets of stone, but on human hearts.**
**— Apostle Paul**

Everybody has needs. You do. I do. So does every donor. Admittedly, there are people who give because the sticker-covered jar is on the convenience store counter and the donor doesn't want to carry a nickel and four pennies in his pocket all day. Of course, that's not the level of giving that will keep your organization thriving. Large donations and repeated donations require great presentations from those who understand the donor's thought process.

The writer of Proverbs quantified this axiom many times and in various ways in his writings: A fool and his money are soon parted. This lets us know that when we are looking for big money from people who have the larger resources, they aren't going to be pushovers or fools. They have battled the battalions of idiots that have tried to relieve them of their resources before, and they have won. Your approach to those of intellect and income must accompany a prowess of donor knowledge. The foundation of any presentation starts when we understand what a donor wants from our organization. It is fundamental. Every donor has seven needs and, depending on the donor, sometimes a few more.

## SEVEN DONOR NEEDS

1.  **Need a clear articulation and understanding of the situation or need.**
    1.  We must articulate the need in a way that touches their heart deeply.

2. We must present the need showing a clear solution.

3. Knowing that people like to support victories rather than defeat, we never ask people to support an unwinnable battle.

## 2. Need to be inspired to be a part of the solution.

1. We must inspire them to believe their contribution will provide the solution.

2. We must sell the importance of their personal involvement.

## 3. Need a clear, unwavering cost for the solution.

1. Find a need that matches the donor's giving potential.

2. Set a clear dollar amount and do not waver.

3. Never use ambiguous phrases like, "We need about ten thousand dollars" or "Hopefully we can do this for ten thousand dollars." Know the cost of success.

4. **Need confidence in you and your organization to complete the task.**

    1. Your look, your speech, and your business plan must illuminate your ability to fully accomplish the task.

    2. Share the victories your organization has seen in lowering county-wide abortion rates, ability to provide public school presentations. Chart past victories.

    3. Mention influential local donors who have supported your work.

    4. The credibility of your board members should help bring credibility to your organization.

5. **Need to receive personal invitation to be a part.**

    1. Ask for the gift. There comes a time in your presentation that you need to get to the reason for your presentation. Ask for the money.

    2. Don't be afraid to challenge people in their giving. Faith is often required to see the hand

of God. Those who trust God will find Him faithful.

3. Ask unashamedly. Don't apologize for asking people to save lives. If you're embarrassed to ask for support, find a worthy cause you can believe in.

6. **Need to be thanked thoroughly and properly.**

   1. Follow up immediately with a handwritten thank you note for any gift over fifty dollars. Large gifts might be worthy of a plaque of thanksgiving.

   2. Continue to find ways to remind the donor how important their gift was with follow-up calls. A donor should be thanked at least three times for their gift, maybe more.

7. **Need to be provided with proof the project was completed.**

   1. Rapidly provide proof that you completed the project they funded.

   2. Send weekly updates if the project is known to be an extended time.

3. Avoid talking about delays or cost overages (ask for 20% more than you need).

4. Talk about gratitude and success. Thank them again.

Though not needed for an initial gift or a repeat gift, your donor will develop more rapidly in support of your organization as you find ways to include them in your inner circle of partners. The "Need to be included" could be thought of as an eighth donor need. The inclusion factor moves your donor from that of a donor to that of a partner in the work.

Remind your donors often how they are the star of the successful projects. The more you make your donor feel responsible for the project's success, the more you'll receive in the future from that financial partner. That holds true for larger and smaller donors.

Find ways to connect with them outside of a fundraising ask. Host lady partner tea times and key partner dinner fellowships. Utilize a mid-year Laugh for Life Comedy Friend-Raiser event. Invite their children to celebrate with them at these Laugh for Life events. Introduce new donors to old donors.

Network - network - network. Your partners will create their own peer pressure for greater challenges when you excite them to action together.

Consider those directors I asked to sell me on giving to their organization in ninety seconds. I want to tell you why most failed horribly and why two succeeded. Most failed because they weren't prepared to clearly articulate the need, inspire the listener to action, or ask for the gift. Failure to prepare is failure.

**People don't buy WHAT you do,
they buy WHY you do it.
— Simon Sinek, Start with Why**

I sat across the dinner table from the owner of a rather successful car dealership. As a relatively known Christian, I am sure that he is "touched" by every charity seeking to save the community, the state, or even the planet. I mentally rehearsed what I believed would set our organization apart from others. As a successful businessman, he was going to be interested in seeing if my business model is simply to pray and wait or if there's wise activity driving our work. As a successful steward, he was going to be interested in the genuine, provable, quantifiable results of any gift he might bestow. Nobody wants to stand at the judgement, having given God half of their fortune through a charity, only to find out that money went to financial failures or shysters.

I approached him with the following basic donor-targeted conversation. I happened to know that every year, he gave large amounts of money to another organization that claims a pro-life world can be achieved through legislation. My job that night was to convince him that our organization was where his money would most successfully be used if he wanted to actually save the life of a real child.

Look again at the first five donor needs and see if you can identify any of them being met in my short presentation to him.

1. They need a clear understanding of the situation / need.

2. They need to be inspired to be a part of the solution.

3. They need a clear, unwavering cost of the situation solution.

4. They need confidence in you or your organization to complete the task.

5. They need to be personally asked to meet that need.

At this point in the conversations, we had already talked about our shared concern with abortion rates, what was going on in world news, and our personal faith story. Tom was as opposed to and appalled by the local abortion numbers as any man could be. He had a heart for the unborn. That didn't need to be developed. Tom needed to see the local PRC as the place where his funding would do the most good.

"Tom, let me have three uninterrupted minutes to present my case to you. And by the way, I think you know Jerry Smith from Nationwide Tractor and Ethan Taylor from Edward-Jones. They have spoken highly of you. They sit on our oversight board. Jerry wanted to come to our meeting today but had to go out of town.

"Tom, I know you must receive hundreds of requests for support every year. Some surely come with a much nicer dinner than we have here. It seems like every generous person gets their name put on a charity hit list somewhere.

"Tom, I want to give you a scenario. Instead of simply selling Ford products, would you be interested in setting up an ad campaign to get the government to force all car buyers to buy a Ford? Think about the ramifications of that. Could it happen? Sure, all we need to do is get eighty percent of our nation's populous to buy into that—or a presidential mandate. Now, while we're waiting for the state government to promote our agenda, a lot of people are buying Chevys, Toyotas, and Hondas.

"This is where our illustration turns to the reality of the Pregnancy Resource Center work. Tom, we aren't spending millions of dollars annually to buy political votes to try and outvote the immoral majority of the people. We know that making something illegal doesn't stop anything. Look at the drug epidemic we have in our country, yet it's illegal.

"The pregnancy center fights for the lives of children a different way. We use brilliant advertising strategies and social media to bring abortion-minded and abortion-vulnerable women through our doors. Then we provide them with the truth about life. We open our doors and actually rescue babies.

"We've been able to rescue over five hundred babies in the eleven years that we've been open. We've seen the transformation of thousands of families through our parenting skills educational programs. Along the way, we even help those who've had past abortions find healing and a place to start again. Amid these services, we're able to introduce them to a personal faith in God and often to a local church.

"There are a lot of good people doing good work in our community, but this is the only place that makes a promise that your gift will save actual lives from death. This ministry snatches little children's lives from the jaws of the abortionist.

"Tom, I want you to be a part of a pro-life ministry that is victorious. I need ten thousand dollars to rescue the next ten children who come through our doors in the belly of mothers who are looking for an abortion. Can I count on you to be the one to save those ten children?"

Now, let's create a meeting scenario with another Tom who is not an automotive dealer and not politically driven. Maybe we know very little about our imaginary Tom #2 and his wife. As we look at an alternate yet very similar presentation, we continue to see our donor needs being met.

"Tom and Janet, this last year seventy-five thousand children in our own state were aborted, tragically terminated. Seventy-five thousand minds that could have held the cure for cancer or the answer to world peace. Two thousand of those children were aborted after twenty-one weeks in the womb. At twenty-one weeks, they are a viable, independent child. Four thousand of those children were aborted right here in our local area. That sickens me. I'm sure it does you, as well.

"Let me tell you about a wonderfully successful program that is combatting those awful numbers. The Pregnancy Resource Center succeeds—yes, succeeds—in substantially lowering those numbers each year. We open our door and advertise like crazy, and in some pretty interesting ways, God brings pregnant girls through our doors. Some, in fact, inadvertently enter our doors thinking they can get an abortion at our center. That's great. We will gladly take any cases of mistaken identity to save the life of a child, amen? God brings them in and we show them an ultrasound—a live movie starring their own baby that proves there is more than a blob of tissue in their stomach. Upon seeing that, ninety-three percent of these girls decide to choose life.

"Then we involve the girls and their husbands in classes that teach them how to be a good mother and a good father. We disciple them. In the fatherless and motherless world, we build families. Most of them didn't have a good family role model, so they don't know how to be a good mother or father. The

Pregnancy Center literally changes the local society by turning a tragedy into a triumph.

It costs us $719 to rescue one child from an abortion-minded client. That is a gift of $1.97 a day. I want to personally ask you and your spouse to join the others in our town who have committed to saving one child or a few children this year. I am here to ask you to be part of our life-saving team. Through the Options for Women Pregnancy Center, you can know that your pro-life stance has accounted for lives saved for eternity. Are you ready to know that your family saved a life this year? Can I put you down to save one child or even two children this year? How can I thank you for being part of our team and part of the winning solution?"

Notice that my last line made it appear that I wasn't questioning the forthcoming gift. I present with full expectation they will join our team. I ask them to be part and move toward thanking them for the first time. Immediately congratulate them for being lifesavers.

Note that the life-saving amounts you use will be based on your center's costs.

**People will forget what you said. They will forget what you did. But they will never forget how you made them feel.**
**— Maya Angelou**

Let's look at the sixth and seventh very important continuing needs your donor has.

6. They need to be thanked thoroughly and properly.

7. They need to be provided with proof the project was completed.
Thank the donor in the closing of your presentation. Then, keep it up until they give again and start the thanking process all over. How many times do we need to thank a donor? I don't know, but I do know that you can never thank a donor too much. In all my years of helping people raise money, I've never had a donor stop giving because they were over-thanked. I have seen donors stop because they didn't feel properly connected.

Board members need to personally call and thank any large donors. The director gets paid to thank people, but a board member call is special. Considering that the average, successful non-profit board member dedicates four hours a week to their treasured organization, this should not be a problem.

**In good times and bad, we know that people give because you meet needs,
not because you have needs.
— Kay Sprinkel Grace**

Sometimes the seventh donor need looks impossible, as the task we are asking them to complete may be a building project that will take a year to complete, but you can provide weekly updates. If they are sponsoring a mother and child, send them a picture of the next child born at your center with a thank you note from the birth mother (write the letter for her). Find a way to provide tangible proof their gift mattered and the organizational promise is being fulfilled.

If you don't use their money for the requested purpose, give the money back or ask permission to use it another way. Some have placed strategic statements in their material noting that all unused gifts will go to the area of most need.

## TAKEAWAY:

When you can fulfill the Seven Donor Needs (+1), you're going to see an amazing increase in dollars given. When you can bring these axioms into every area of your presentations, you'll see marked increase in your WALK dollars, your Golf Tournament dollars, your Baby Bottle Boomerang dollars, your underwriting, and your banquet donations. These fundraising axioms work in every area of presentation. Meet your donors' needs and you'll open the floodgates of blessing as you see God join you in your wisdom and work.

# 2

## Start Your Own Millionaires Club

**Zaccheus, come down from that tree, I am going to your house today, and we are going to eat. Get ready to lighten your wallet.**
**— Jesus Christ**

Zaccheus stood barely five feet tall in his designer-made, high-lift sandals. The least popular man in Jericho was a leading tax collector for Rome. In doing so, he got very rich himself. Jesus could have settled with allowing him to be in the crowd of listeners—as he was—just like everybody else. But for some reason, Jesus called him out, called him down, and invited Himself and His entire board (the disciples) over to his house. Why didn't Jesus deal with the wealthy guy in the same way as the normal guy? I could answer, but it would be purely theological speculation.

Although it is not needed for an initial gift, donor inclusion will certainly bring you increased revenue as you move forward in your quest for future gifts.

**Donors need to feel included in the family circle of the organization.**

Call it "The Inclusion Factor" if you must. It is perhaps the most overlooked of the donor need items if you want to move that good donor to a great donor status. If I only called you once a year, and when I did it was to ask you for money, how would you feel about our relationship? You would find it rather one-sided. You might stop taking my calls, believing I considered you a mark on my fundraising belt. We must love and nurture our donors often, at times without asking for a dime. We need to let them come together as a donor family to celebrate the victories they have funded. Have a victory dinner for your larger-tier donors. Let them encourage each other in greater giving. Peer pressure will bring you greater gifts. And for the record, you need to truly love your donors. Don't fake it.

Consider inviting your high-level donors to a smaller yearly banquet (separate from your normal banquet)—a get together in a private restaurant room where you share intimately about the future of your organization and ask these higher level donors to be a big part. Larger money appreciates the exclusivity that comes from special attention. These larger donors will encourage each other to give more. They may even start an out-giving war with each other. How tragically wonderful.

**If we don't connect with our donors, you can bet your last donation that there will be a charity who will.**
**— Terica Williams**

A few years ago, I saw a great need in the Pregnancy Resource Center world. I saw yearly fundraising banquets with nothing in between. Some would remind me of their 5K Walk and the 7Ks and their NO-K Golf Tournament, but not often. Those are great alternative fundraising additions to your banquet, but they are usually comprised of people who aren't your normal banquet partners. The banquet—usually your highest dollar-raising event— is primarily made up of people you only shake hands with once a year. And how did you feel about that one-time-a-year call that was only to ask you for a large gift?

Think about your own banquet. We all know that repeat attendance at stewardship events is extremely unstable. Every year some centers see as much as a sixty-percent turnover in attendees. You can't build a secure financial foundation with that kind of apathetic repetition. I have gone places where board members can't seem to make it to the banquet. Shocking. We need to have alternative get-togethers for fellowship and personal touch. Without those alternative connections, we will become charitably invisible.

I preface the following by telling you that there are multiple ways to do what I am calling a Friend-Raiser other than the seemingly self-serving illustration I will use. Although I do believe that the track record will show this to be the best one in use.

A few years ago, in grieving these yearly attendance turnovers and desiring to bring new donors to our PRC table, I united three talented guys and launched Laugh for Life Friend-Raiser Events. Laugh for Life is a mid-year—opposite your banquet—event to bring your donors and their entire family to laugh and celebrate the victories being seen by your center.

Centers have their special donors come early and meet (dine or snack with) the comedian. They open it up to the community to bring in new friends to hear about the ministry. The director shares the ministry (a lot like we shared with our real Tom or our created Tom and Janet) and then the comedian makes the crowd laugh hard for forty minutes. Then the comedian tells about the success of the organization and they receive a soft-sell offering, reminding the audience that many in the room are already monthly supporters and honoring them with applause. "If you have given a financial gift to the

PRC at the banquet this last year or participated in our Walk for Life please stand. Give these wonderful lifesavers an enormous, thunderous hand. They are amazing!"

Then a prize drawing is taken from the offering envelopes for a complete set of the comedian's material, which has been donated by the comedian. The information received from the collection envelopes—names with donation amounts—gives you a list of potential invitees for your next yearly banquet. Extremely generous friend-raiser donors get invitations to your next stewardship event and maybe even a personal visit or personal invitation for a center tour. This Friend-Raiser event takes about twelve total man hours to arrange and usually garners a net gain of a few thousand dollars, a few new monthly donors, and a new list of special people who your center will personally invite to the banquet, subsequently turning them into great monthly partners.

I could have united some great musician friends for this event. I've worked and toured with them for the last twenty-five years. But I know that music is the most divisive event in the church. We all like a certain genre of music, and many consider all other genres to be substantially less than sacred. In fact, you're more likely to split a church over a change in music style than you are in a doctrinal shift. Many have found that comedy is a wonderful way to unite the age groups, including Millennials (your future), in the donor-bonding experience.

**Abortion is not funny, but saving children from abortion, which is what we do, is the most joyful thing a person can do. Laugh loud … life wins! And nobody does it better than the local PRC.**
**— Gordon Douglas**

Those who don't understand why you would use comedy to represent a serious subject have never watched a Jerry Lewis Labor Day Telethon. Some unknowing boards fear using comedy under the thought of "How can you talk about abortion and laugh?" That's a good point if you were an organization that was performing abortions. But you aren't. You're saving lives, and that is something to celebrate with joy and laughter. When you understand what moves people, you'll understand why comedy has been the number one PRC fundraiser for many years.

You can meet the guys who do these friend-raiser events at LaughForLife.us and learn a lot about how to better create an alternative friend-raising event from the material contained there. This is one way to help fulfill the eighth after-gift donor need. Get creative. Connect!

## TAKEAWAY:

You must connect with your donors in ways that are in addition to your yearly banquet event. Find ways to bring new people to your doors while bringing fellowship to your consistent donors. You must bring your donors into the inner sanctum of trust and friendship through relationship. Upon doing so, they will become lifetime donors. Schedule lunches with your donors to do nothing more than eat and share testimonies. Are your board members doing this too? Did I hear laughter? Directors must model this for their boards and require their boards to participate.

Schedule one evening each week to call your donors to ask them how they are doing. Crazy, you say? Maybe, maybe not.

# 3

## I Can Only Listen for Eight Seconds

**Work, for the night is coming when no man can work.**
**— Jesus Christ**

John Maxwell says, "In the end, people are persuaded not by what we say, but by what they understand." I want to amend Dr. Maxwell's quote to remind you that we are living in a world of short-attention-span theater. In this world, where seventy percent of the inhabitants have ADD or ADHD, we must bring attention and understanding of our issue at breakneck speed. A story that can be told quickly can be heard quickly, understood more fully, responded to more easily, and face fewer distractions. These days, it seems that every two minutes we're interrupted by a text, a tweet, or a cell phone call. Sometimes the challenges to my presentations are not in getting an appointment, but rather in finding the free seconds during that appointment when my future donor isn't distracted by some other incoming communique. I've considered bringing a cell phone jammer to presentations. Yes, they're available. Get one for your counseling rooms too.

Have you ever put a stopwatch on a television commercial? The average commercial has been thirty seconds long for the last forty years. That's changing. Look at the commercials now. They're clocking in at fifteen seconds. In those fifteen seconds, an advertising agency is telling a story and completing an ask. Wow. That's good. If they can do it, we can too. Let's learn from the professional advertisers.

**First there is the 10-second war: can you do something in your first moments on stage to ensure people's eager attention**

**while you set up your talk topic? Second is the 1-minute war: can you then use that first minute to ensure that they're committed to coming on the full talk journey with you?**
**— Chris J. Anderson, TED Talks: The Official TED Guide to Public Speaking**

We are in a world of high-speed everything. It may have started in 1945, when the microwave oven taught the American public that their food preparation time was far too long. "We demand popcorn in three minutes." Now the average American will exit any web search if the page doesn't load in under eight seconds. We're an impatient society. Why? I don't know. Do we need the extra time so we can have more time to do other things real fast? Your ability to keep the attention of younger audiences and older audiences will be determined by your ability to give your message clearly and in a very short window of time.

I love TED Talks. The TED Talks presentation dynasty has called for people to give the speech of their life in eighteen minutes, and then they electronically deliver that speech around the world through their network. Eighteen-minute speeches are the new norm. Pastors who once spoke for an hour now have parishioners and deacons alike walking out after eighteen minutes. Maybe that is why any sermon of Jesus can be read, even slowly, in less than three minutes. Maybe Jesus knew something we've been missing. Less is often more. By the time many of us determine the focus level of a listener, they have reached the end of their ability to focus.

**Despite Mike's inability to write a short book, he really does understand the Less is More principle in his presentations.**
**— Terica Williams**

You need to articulate a story, share a testimony, or give an illustration as part of any presentation quickly. You can do that quickly if you start with the end in mind.

Let's do a self-evaluation. Imagine I'm a potential donor and we've just finished a wonderful lunch. We talked about my family, and you threw in a few points of connection to your life and family. You've told me of the others in my sphere of influence who support your organization. You've told me what a thrill it is for you to be working at a successful organization. We are connecting on a personal, friendly level. In one very simple sentence, out loud, articulate a dollar amount that you want to see me give as a result of our meeting.

You might say, "Mike, I need you to provide $25,000 for a new ultrasound machine. How can we make this happen? What information can I share to move you to be the one who brings life to over ninety percent of our clients for the next five years?"

You might say, "Mike, I need you to become a $1.97 a day donor. Yes, $59-a-month donor, and you can know that you are personally saving one child this year. How can we make this happen? What information can I provide you with right now for you to see the need and personally desire to meet that need?"

Go back and read both of those ask sentences a few times. Say them louder and more boldly each time. Say them until they roll off your tongue as easily as saying the names of your children and with the same shameless attitude. You may think this is silly, but until you can quickly ask for funding as easily as you say your name, your mind will stall at this point in your presentation. Learn to boldly and rapidly speak out your financial request. We are not embarrassed to ask people to join a God work.

Sales trainers say the difference between a good salesman and a great one is their ability to ask for money at the end of a presentation. That sounds silly. We all know that. Of course we do, but if you fail to turn the information in this book into funding, it will most likely be because of that one great hurdle: asking.

Your desire in a fundraising presentation is funding, right? Let's keep that "funding" word in our mind as we move forward. Constantly remind yourself that your goal is "funding" in every presentation. I asked the great fundraising humorist Paul Aldrich how he prepared for his presentations, and in his always witty and honest style he replied, "I like to work ask-backwards." He prepared to ask for the money first, and then added only the words that were absolutely necessary to achieve that goal. He took out anything that did not directly relate to the culminating point of asking for money. That is good advice. That is wisdom.

In preparation for writing your own presentation, you must remember and fulfill those basic donor needs within your presentation. Anything less than that is failure on your part. This is why so many big-name sports figures and celebrities are such horrible fundraisers. Sometimes they can draw a crowd, but they are often unable to successfully encourage the crowd to give their hard-earned money to the organization they were paid dearly to represent. Celebrities and celebrities' family members, no matter how good their stories are, are rarely trained fundraisers. This does not mean we throw them out. They are great for your non-fundraising connection events. Use them for those.

**Give me a great unknown presenter and twenty listeners over a celebrity and two hundred listeners any day. The great presenter will win every time.**
**— Jack Eason**

As we keep in mind what we know about the needs the donor, I want you to begin to construct your own super-effective ask presentation. We are going for effectiveness, not eloquence here.

Think about the words:
Captivating - Contemplating - Cultivating

Think about the words:
Inspirational - Informational - Invitational

Your own presentation must include some key ingredients if you hope to secure a great donation. First, you must present a captivating, inspirational reason that I should listen to your pitch and not be distracted by the text arriving on my cell phone as we speak. Captivating is just that—captivating. I spent the better part of three weeks trying different titles for this very book that buyers would find captivating. I asked a lot of friends to share with me what captivating sentence they believed would inspire you to drop eighteen dollars down on this book. We must have settled on the right title—at least for you.

**If a speaker, any speaker, does not captivate me in the first few seconds of their presentation, they will spend the rest of their talk trying to get me back on board their train.**
**— Ken Davis**

When I first started to develop this system, I was trying to get the basic presentation outline down to three words. Three is a great amount of anything. I was using the words inspirational, informational, and invitational. Inspirational wasn't a strong enough word to convey what I was trying to teach. When you make a presentation, from the first moment you open your mouth, you need to say something that wakes people up and commands the attention of the room. As a speaker, I know that if I don't win the audience over in the first thirty seconds, I will spend the rest of the night trying to regain their attention.

**Good is the enemy of great.**
**— Voltaire (updated)**

It was after ten grueling nights of back-to-back 4 a.m. wake-up calls, I was exhausted—almost asleep—at my beautiful Hampton Inn when the television news reporter made a statement that so interested me I couldn't continue going to sleep. It was one single statement that was so captivating I had to stay awake and hear the story, so I sat wide awake for twenty minutes waiting for it to come on. I realized halfway through the story that it wasn't the story I was supposed to hear. It was this illustration. We need to speak in a way that captivates our listener. Give your listener a reason to listen.

**Captivating is not "It is good to be here tonight." Captivating is "There is an insane man with a gun outside this door, and I can tell you the only way out." Now everyone in your room really wants to hear you.**
**— Terica Williams**

I remember the rather unruly and distracted audience at the large, Woodstock-style Jesus festival. There must have been thirty thousand people milling around and talking as if they could not care less about the speaker coming on. They were waiting for the next big Christian band to lead them to Jesus as the short, squat, bald, sweating speaker took the stage. He paced back and forth and blurted into the microphone, "Thirty-five thousand children will die today of fixable causes, and most of you don't give a damn about it." The crowd went quiet, if for nothing more than his choice of adjectives at a religious event. "And the worst thing is that in this group of Christians, most of you are more concerned with the fact that I used the word damn than you are the thirty-five thousand children who will die. That breaks the heart of God." He now had us under his verbal control. Every one of us. Like him, love him, hate him, he had our attention. Like him, love him, hate him, we hung on his every single word to see what this communicator could possibly say next. By the way, hundreds of people sponsored a child in a third-world mission program that night after his inconsiderate, ungodly, uncouth, unforgivable presentation. The speaker gave us a reason to listen and not go to the snack shack while we waited for Third Day to get the amplifiers ready to rock.

Be true to your internal personality while finding a way to be captivating. Going that far with an older audience might make them unable to ever get past your use of what they consider to be unforgivable profanity. A Millennial audience might find that kind of statement relevant and attractive. Consider your audience as you consider your captivating opening. Speak to the money in the room and not extremes.

**Think of your captivating presentation like you would speed dating.**
**You've only got six minutes. You better look good, smell good, and sound good. You also better work in the fact that you have a secure future or you might not get a second six minutes.**
**— Paul Aldrich**

Every time I step onto a fundraising platform or give a personal financial appeal, I go through a ritual. I go back through the basics of what I will need to share with the audience based on the information I know about the organization. Here is my own simple SIX-R preparation formula that I created to prepare myself to deliver a financially successful presentation. I use this outline no matter how long or short my presentation time will be. It's not about the time; it's about the content.

**Reason:** Captivate your audience with an emotion-touching story or illustration that draws the potential listener into the presentation and moves the listener to demand to be part of the story. Wake them out of a dead sleep with your opening sentence. Show the horrendous problem or amazing victory in a way that moves them deeply. Anything less is a failure on our part. It is our responsibility to interest the listener, not the listener's responsibility to find us interesting.

**Response:** Don't captivate me with a problem unless you can also excite me with a solution. Anyone can talk about a problem. Tell me how "you and I together" are the solution to the problem.

**Results:** Convince me of your ability to successfully perform that response and complete that solution. Share your past results in numbers of children rescued and families transformed from at-risk to thriving. Prove that you are an effective remedy for the opening statement. This seems kind of silly to even have to say, but if you believe that children are individual people, count them in your stats.

**Remind:** Remind the donor of your shared vision and passion to solve the problem. Develop a camaraderie of ideology and resolve through your articulate conversation. Bring credibility by listing other influential people who believe in and support the work.

**Request:** You have to ask to receive. Ask. Ask the listener to be part of the success story. Expect a yes! If you can't in good conscience ask them to be a part, find someone who can.

**Receive:** Receive the gift in the way the donor chooses. Be prepared to actually take the money.

Let's look at a presentation using this SIX-R outline. The following one was designed to be presented within a two- to three-minute timeline.

## SAMPLE ASK PRESENTATION #1

**Reason:** "Last year, in our tri-county area, twenty-four thousand children were senselessly terminated in their mothers' wombs—many because their mothers had been led to believe they were simply a blob of meaningless tissue. Three hundred of those beautiful babies were over twenty-one weeks of age—old enough to easily survive outside the womb, on their own, at the very time of their termination." (Note that we shrunk the abortion scale to our local area and dug deeper with the late-term information.)

**Response:** "Our center uses a modern business approach to capture the attention of abortion-minded and abortion-vulnerable women, showing them the truth about their pregnancy through our ultrasound and personal counseling. That combination gives us a ninety-seven percent success rate with every woman we see. We have a solution to this crisis, and we can save more." (Notice how we assured them we were efficient and had a successful business model.)

**Results:** "Last year alone we were able to rescue 356 children and equip the mothers and fathers through our Parenting Skills University. We were able to do this at a cost of only $1.97 a day for each child rescued." (Notice how we limited the scope of our service listing to link only with the services that affected our opening captivating need. We replaced "Earn While You Learn" with "Parenting Skills

University," a term that did not need to be explained. We also introduced a very reasonable cost figure to be part of the solution.)

**Remind:** "I know that you believe in saving lives as much as I do. I also know there are many groups pulling for your pro-life partnership. Here is our promise: we will not spend one dime of your money on unsuccessful political promises. We will, however, rescue children in your name and transform their family through our educational programs." (Notice how we assure them that we know they care about this situation and expect they would want to help. We also exclaim that we will do this in their name, for them.)

**Request:** "I know these tragic statistics bother you as much as they do me. I also know that you're as excited about the victories we're having as I am. This is why I'm personally asking you—right now—to be part of the cure. Can I count on you to share $1.97 a day to know your family has personally rescued one child? Perhaps you want to join those partners who are sponsoring the rescue of a number of children. How can we count on you?" (Notice how we honed in on one possible giving amount and showed the results of that gift, explaining in minimal wording how their family could be part of a genuinely life-changing result. When seeking a large gift, go right to the big number. "We need twenty-five thousand dollars to expand the center to serve 100 more children a month. Can I count on you?")

**Receive:** "Some of our partners choose to give monthly, while others give us a single check. We are set up to receive gifts through credit cards. That's what I use. I like the extra air miles/points I receive. How can we best serve you in your beautifully generous, life-saving gift?"

Unless you set up some sort of agreement as to the payment timeline, you have not successfully completed your presentation. When asking for single large gifts, you will not have to supply payment options, as most larger givers will not need payment plans.

Most of the gracious executive directors and development directors who allowed me that interview question, if they were able to say anything, launched into how they do what they do without ever telling me the captivating reason why they do it. Only one director—none of the development directors— actually asked me for the money as they closed their pitch. Most of them simply ended their talk and smiled as if my wallet would open by osmosis and a pro cignod, blank chock would magically float heavenward.

If I were an executive director, I would call my development director right now and ask the interview question, as you need to know if the person you are paying to ask for you really knows how to do it effectively. If I were a development director, I would ask my ED that question to see if they were, as the voice of the center, prepared to answer this request. If not, prepare them.

Let me briefly remind you of that initial premise/situation question: We are on an elevator, and I ask you to tell me why I should give you the ten thousand dollars in my pocket and not the guy on the twenty-second floor. In the two bad presentation examples below, you will find a synopsis of what my ED and DD respondents said.

## BAD PRESENTATION EXAMPLE #1

"We need your money because we have a lot of programs that we do, like Earn-While-You-Learn and Post-abortive Bible Studies, and the cost of rent, as you well know, is very high in our community. We do some school abstinence programs—not as many as we would like to do because schools are hard to get into, and we lost our presenter last year—but we really want to get back into that. Last year we did 123 pregnancy tests and 64 ultrasounds. We gave away over 10,000 diapers, and most of those were donated to us by the local community or churches and private individuals who know us and love our work. Oh, and the food bank helps us too. We provide bassinets, layettes, wipes, lotion, and formula for lots of pregnant girls in our area. We give away pre-natal vitamins too. We are sponsored by over twenty churches in the area, and a lot business people also contribute. Oh yes, and the local thrift store gives us their excess baby clothing. So, that's what we do. Does that answer your question?"

I can answer our presenter's last question with a resounding "No." This failed presentation told me very little about why I should support you. It was about as captivating to me as the unfinished episodes of I lannah Montana. It drew me into nothing passionate and broke a very huge rule: never lead with money or services. Lead with a captivating need or situation (story) that your organization can solve with their help. This response left me without understanding of the need or how a donor would meet it and asked for no specific gift amount. It also made the center look like a large welfare organization in a world that is growing ever-opposed to more welfare programs. My own middle-class children can barely afford disposable diapers. They're having to use cloth and you're giving them away? Earning the diapers wasn't articulated—not that it should have been—but the presenter did bring it up. I didn't hear about the impact on public school through the sexual integrity classes, when you did do them (The past is the past.). I heard your test count, but how effective were those? How many babies did you save last year? Or better yet, since you have been open? This presentation gave few, if any, credibility statements. I was told that people were giving you a lot of diapers already, so my help was not needed for that. I know very little about this organization other than the fact that the leader cannot articulate why they should be in existence and why I need to be a financial part of it.

**We need to know the WHY, before the WHAT and before the HOW.**

**Very few people or companies can clearly articulate WHY they do WHAT they do. When I say WHY, I don't mean to make money— that's a result. By WHY I mean what is your purpose, cause or belief? WHY does your company exist? WHY do you get out of bed every morning? And WHY should anyone care?**
**—Simon Sinek, Start with Why**

## BAD PRESENTATION EXAMPLE #2

"There were 1.2 million abortions in our country last year. It is running rampant and we intend to stop it. We provide pregnancy tests and limited ultrasound verifications and parenting training. Last year, we gave away over 14,000 diapers, held a 5K Walk, a Golf Tournament, and a Baby-Bottle-Boomerang, which brings in a tremendous amount of money. We provided services and supplies for over 1,200 clients this year. We also presented in seven area schools. We are open three days a week, from ten to four and every other Friday from nine to twelve. Our girls come from all over the county. Sixty-two percent are African-American, twenty-two percent are Hispanic, and the remainder are white, but many of those have an ethnic father. We offer services in Spanish one day a week when we can. This is our fourth year of operation but our first year in the new office that was renovated by local churches and volunteers. Our biggest need is more room."

The organization is a local one. Keep the facts local, not national. Be honest, a PRC is not trying to overturn abortion laws. If you are, you're going about it all wrong. A PRC is a local life-saving station. Be the victorious life-saving station and not another unsuccessful political action group. The 5K Walk or the Golf Tournament have no persuasive pull on anyone giving you money? I don't know what a Baby-Bottle-Boomerang is, and if it was so successful, why am I being asked for money? What kind of success was achieved with 1,200 clients? What was presented at seven schools, and was it effective? Your open hours told me you're only interested in rescuing babies from people who were unemployed. Your ethnicity report led me to feel that you mainly serve one demographic, not mine. This presentation asked for no specific financial gift that would solve the 1.2 million abortions problem you alluded to solving. If it did, the amount would be staggering, as the cost of rescuing 1.2 million children might be beyond the resources of most donors, unless you're talking to Bill Gates. How will my predetermined financial amount save X amount of lives or provide X services to meet a believable goal or solve a passionate dilemma? Give me a need I can meet, a cost to meet it, and ask me to meet the need now. This presentation did not ask me to give money. Maybe your biggest need is more hours than it is more room. That is simple business math. However, never say the biggest need is anything but $$ when you are doing a fundraising pitch.

The SIX-R outline shows that you can make a great presentation in two minutes. In fact, you can reduce most financial presentations (or any other story) to as few as five focused phrases when you start with the end in mind.

Look at how one hugely successful movie studio quantizes their story for production:

Once upon a time there was a fish named Marlin, a widower who was very protective of his only son, Nemo.

Every day, Marlin repeatedly warned Nemo about the dangers of the ocean and warned him not to stray far from home.

One day, in an act of independence, Nemo ignored those warnings and swam out into the open water.

Because of that, Marlin sets off on a rescue mission, receiving the help of other sea creatures along the way.

Finally, today Marlin and Nemo reunite, celebrate, and reminisce in lessons well learned.

That is how five simple phrases can be used to summarize a ninety-minute movie. Can you summarize a five-minute story the same way? I think you can.

Feel free to get boisterous and prideful as you share the "Because of That" success story phrases of your center. Success can never be understated. People want to join a winning team. Get to the problem quick, get to the solution quick, prove your ability boldly, then ask. Sometimes you might use your "Because of That" line multiple times. Relax, when you are telling any story this fast, you have plenty of time to get bold in your successes.

Look at this quick, fill-in-the-blank way to pre-write your presentation:

Once upon a time: _____

Every day: _____

One day: _____

Because of that: _____

Finally, today: _____

Look at this outline that was submitted at one of our workshops:

**For many years,** the women of our county have been misled to believe that abortion was safe and had no emotional side effects.

**Every day** that lie has continued to build until we now see 21,000 children terminated every year from this county alone, and 1,400 are terminated after they are twenty-one weeks old.

**One day** in 2001, Hope Pregnancy Center was formed and rapidly began going about curbing those stats of death through effective rescue programs.

**Because of that** over 1,800—yes, I said 1,800—babies have been saved from abortion, and their mothers and fathers are being transformed through parenting education classes and ongoing personal counseling. These at-risk families are being transformed into thriving families. This effects our entire community's future. Abstinence education is made available every year in the public schools. We are now serving over 1,200 women and their babies every year and rescuing ninety-two percent of children whose mothers receive an ultrasound at our clinic.

**Now today** with your help, we can rescue another child. Will you rescue, save, give life to one child this year with your gift of $1.97 a day? Can I count on you?

The simple outline above can be used to prepare for any event presentation, fundraising presentation, or testimony. Try it with your own life story. You don't need twenty minutes of setup anymore, and you shouldn't have it either. You are the speaker. You control how long you open your mouth. You control the room. Control it with your captivating, easy-to-listen-to presentation.

I have often heard it said, "I just open my mouth and let the Lord fill it." It's funny how those so-called Lord-filled speeches only lead people to believe that God is boring, disorganized, and unprepared. Why is it that we always take more time to speak than Jesus ever did? Is Jesus more fluent in English today than He was in Aramaic?

Jesus was a short story specialist. He was the innovator of the why story and delivered most of his biblically recorded sermons in record time. His longest sermon can be read entirely in less than three minutes. Does that make you think we who claim to be following His example might start mimicking Him too? Here is a presenter who changed the world by using good works, amazingly short life illustrations, and calling for a response. He didn't start with a list of things His kingdom would need, a list of his effected demographics, or video presentations of His disciples working at the office with a contemporary song playing in the background. He started out by saying, "There was a man who found a treasure." Everyone would like to find a treasure. That is captivating to a poor person. He led with, "Let me tell you a story about ten virgins." I wonder if using the word virgin turned as many heads as it might today? Jesus always called people into a story and asked them to join Him in His work with all their heart. Talk about an ask. He asked for everything.

**IMPERATIVE EXERCISE:**

Take out a piece of paper and write the following three presentations. Using the Six-R outline, write one for a monthly giving presentation and one for a large project presentation. Using the "Once upon a time…" outline write your own personal testimony. Edit - edit - edit. Economize words. Go for brevity. Go for clarity. Find a way to captivate the listener.

The same editing/focus principles apply to your fundraising banquet. What are the distractions in your presentation? Why do you have beautiful, thirty-dollar centerpieces made of fish tanks and diamonds? Do cubic zirconia sparkles and live goldfish move your donor toward your ultimate goal? I can't see a donor saying, "I was going to give you a hundred dollars, but know I'm going to give you five thousand because I like to know that a lot of goldfish will ultimately die because of your pro-life centerpieces." I seem to be thinking like a Millennial here. Even our decorations need to move the donor emotionally or support the end message. Some wisely use 8X10 pictures of children on the table to provide proof of their life-saving success. I love that.

A few years ago, I developed a centerpiece presentation that has become quite popular—a birthday cake (or cupcake) display with one candle. Along with a wonderful reading that goes with it, the audience sings "Happy Birthday" to all the children who will hear it sung to them because of the work of the PRC. When done right, the audience will have tears in their eyes. This is not rocket science. It is complete presentation wisdom.

## TAKEAWAY:

Unless your presentation meets the donors' felt needs, you have not really presented at all—you have only talked for a while. You must complete a thorough and rapid presentation to every person you encounter. Not every presentation you do is for financial funding. Sometimes the presentation is for volunteers or board members. The SIX-R outline can be used to meet the felt needs of the donor or future volunteer. The principles are the same, while the stories are different.

As an example, in preparation for writing this book, I started with the following six lines:

**For a long time,** I have watched great ministries failing to achieve their fundraising potential because of one or two easily correctable mistakes in their presentations. Thousands of dollars were alluding them.

**Every night** I sat watching the audience's response, line by line, to every statement made by the directors and the client testimonies. I complained nightly to my wife about the failures and began to take notes regarding the centers who had great failures and great victories.

**One day** I said, "Enough is enough," and I began to put all the information together in a simple-to-understand process. I taught that collected information at national conferences and on personal conference calls with EDs and DDs all over the country. I eventually responded to requests from other Christian organizations to teach the system.

**Because of this,** many organizations began achieving greater income. Some doubled and tripled their income from previous years.

**Finally,** I chose to articulate this simple system in a book so that PRCs and any other ministries can understand these proven principles and raise more money for a God purpose.

I practice what I preach. Go back and do the exercise portion of this chapter right now.

# 4

## But I'm Not a Salesperson

**He who goes forth with passion, spreading from his bag of seed, shall indeed come again with a shout of joy, bringing his harvest with him.**
**— King David**

The Death of a Salesman, Arthur Miller's memorable play, was first performed in 1949. The plot circled around the death of a tired, often depressed, middle-aged salesman named Willy Loman. Willy's less-than-happy life as a salesman had left him crumpled and defeated. His figure made it easy for all of the world to sketch a rather dim view of salespeople. This may be why some people see salespeople as disingenuously smiling characters, constantly looking for some way to "get something over on" whomever they meet. Often these carnival-barking incorrigibles have been known to sell friends and strangers things they don't need and certainly can't afford.

**If I had asked people what they wanted,
they would have said a faster horse.
— Henry Ford**

In truth, the ethical status of a salesperson is not predetermined by their occupation. How we feel about them is directly proportioned to how we feel about their product. Your doctor (a salesperson) tells you how much you need (sells) an operation. It isn't looked at as a way to get into your wallet through your gall bladder. It's looked at as saving your life. You appreciate that medical salesman.

**If you hear a voice within you say "you cannot
paint," then by all means paint, and that voice will
be silenced.
— Vincent Van Gogh**

Your own pastor, a salesperson, sells you on how he interprets the Bible. If he was not a fairly good salesman, you would most likely move to another church. Hopefully he is appreciated for his passion, calling, and persuasive ability. Though some have used their pulpit for selfish gain, most are thoroughly committed to delivering the truth from a heart of love. They are, like Paul the Apostle, biblical salespeople.

**Ants shape each other's behavior by exchanging chemicals. We do it by standing in front of each other, peering into each other's eyes, waving our hands, and emitting strange sounds from our mouths. Human to human.**
**— Chris J. Anderson, TED Talks: The Official TED Guide to Public Speaking**

We are all salespeople. We often choose our clothing based on how we perceive those around us are going to feel about us in that outfit. We choose to bathe and wear deodorant to sell ourselves in relationships to others. We all want to make a good impression, if for no other reason than to sell ourselves. An internet report declared, "People wearing T-shirts are thought of as less intelligent than those in a button-down shirt." This understanding caused me to throw away almost every T-shirt I owned and vow to never wear one outside of my house again. Why? Because of the possible effect it could have on other peoples' perception of my mental prowess, my mission, and my business.

I love the Matthew 15 story involving the problematic woman—at least for the Disciples—who had been following closely and came and knelt before Jesus. "Lord, help my daughter," she said. He replied, "It is not right to take the children's bread and toss it to the dogs." Ouch! This is not the ultra-kind Jesus I learned about in children's church. But don't let that distract you from her response, for His response did not distract her from her sales pitch. She replied, "Yes, Lord, but even the dogs eat the crumbs that fall from their master's table." Then Jesus answered, "Woman, you have great faith. Your request is granted." She pushed in, held fast, and sold it. The Bible says that her daughter was healed from that very hour.

I like this kind of tenacity. I love this kind of unquenchable pushiness for a worthy cause. This is what you need in order to be a great fundraiser for your organization—and for God's kingdom too. We don't get discouraged by insults, and we don't take "no" for an answer.

**Trust begins to emerge when we have a sense that another person or organization is driven by things other than their own self gain.**
**— Simon Sinek, Start with Why**

Don't fear the "salesperson" label. It's another title for development director. That does sound much better, but we know what it really is. When you are good at what you do, whatever that is, you receive the respect you deserve from those around you. People pay large sums of money for these "salespeople" to come to events and ask other people for money. Ironically, the better I get at being the dreaded "salesperson of the cause," the more people want me, and the more they pay. I want to be the best salesperson in the world. What about you?

## TAKEAWAY:

Every great counselor, pastor, coach, or fundraiser is a great salesperson. There is nothing wrong with pushing a product, a theology, or a request for money, as long as what we are selling is genuinely good, honest, and upright. Wear your fundraiser hat as a badge of honor. And be really good!

# 5

## Twenty-five + One = Success

**Still other seed fell on good soil, where it produced a crop—a hundred, sixty, or thirty times what was sown. Whoever has ears, let them hear.**
**— Jesus Christ**

"Never, never, never give up." Churchill issued those immortal words during the German bombardment of Europe. Some people call sales an exercise in determination, tenacity, perseverance, or resolve. I like to think of it as a simple unbiased numbers game.

I am not a math guru. I can add whole numbers without my iPhone. I'm pretty good at money math. I know that one dollar combined with two dollars will equal three dollars, unless you hold it for a while, upon which inflation will make your three dollars worth two dollars. Let me give you a math equation to ponder.

When I was fifteen years old, I sold for a company called Fuller Brush. I could not legally be a Fuller Brush representative at that age, so my wheelchair-bound mom signed up to be a door-to-door salesman, but I was the one who went from door to door. Let me summarize my door-to-door sales time in ten words: If you're smart, you can learn a lot from rejection.

Fast forward to 1990. I embarked on a new career. I was going to be a public speaker. I had attended the Ken Davis Dynamic Communicator (SCORRE) seminar. I even went to his Speaker Summit, where I learned the secrets of making a living as a public speaker. I could do a speech about anything, anywhere, and for any time length. If you needed a speech about how lawn furniture is superior to a Craftmatic adjustable bed, I was your man. I knew how to speak with passion and power and prowess and potential and fourteen other dynamic words that start with P. Shortly after, I found that the people I wanted to turn into clients rejected my wonderful offer, thus rejecting my talent, thus rejecting me. I learned that selling yourself was even harder than selling bottle brushes door to door.

**The difference between average people and achieving people is their perception of and response to failure.**
**— John C. Maxwell**

I found a very helpful formula in the midst of my pursuits. I realized that out of every one hundred calls, I would get four people to say yes to my offer to speak at their event. Sometimes I would make ninety calls before I would get one yes, but before I would get to one hundred, I would have four checks in the win-win category. Do the math and fractions here. On average, every twenty-five calls were victorious. I taught myself to look at every "not interested" as one step closer to a win-win.

I learned to look at each of the twenty-four steps to my next booking as practice, to perfect my pitch for step number twenty-five. I believe in practice. Paul Burton, a corporate legal training specialist and time management instructor says, "It is not 'practice makes perfect,' but practice until you can't get it wrong." Each of my steps to victory became, and should become for you, a happy repetition of perfecting the craft. If you look at it that way—and continue to—you will find your success mathematics will serve your mental health much better.

**An innovator who has brilliant ideas but lacks the discipline and persistence to carry them out is merely a dreamer.**
**— Malcomb Gladwell**

It's interesting as I look back on the groups that once rejected my services. Now they're on a waiting list to receive my services a year from now and at a cost of many times my earlier rates. Because I treated their rejection with respect, we can both look back and laugh about it. I had to realize those were not eternal rejections. They were just postponements of win-win situations for next year. So with that in mind, you really should book me now for your next fundraising event. You may not be able to afford me in two more years.

A "no" today does not mean a "no" tomorrow. Be faithful to present with passion and integrity and see the results come to pass. How long must a child try to walk before he actually does so? A child would never ask the question, for the answer does not matter. Keep calm and sell on.

## TAKEAWAY:

If you are going to raise funds, get ready for rejections. Don't take it personally. Share all seven donor need steps, share the captivating talk, and give your best ask by the numbers. Accept each rejection with joy, knowing that you are now only one—or twenty-five—more calls, visits, or dinners away from phenomenal success. Never, never, never give up. Your persistence will give you great rewards. I believe you have what it takes.

# 6

## Carpe Diem

**Be very careful, then, how you live—not as unwise but as wise, making the most of every opportunity, because the days are evil.**
**— Apostle Paul**

As I prepared to write, I prayed. I prayed for wisdom and creativity from God. I do this most every day. As I closed my calendar this morning, a little blurb on the front page of my AT-A-GLANCE monthly planner caught my eye. Yes, I still like a paper calendar to back up the electronic. On the info page, it says this:

You've got appointments to make, places to go, and commitments to keep.
You have big plans—plans that guide your future.
When you write it down, you make it happen.
**It's your life. Take note.**

I'm sure this is some kind of company motto or sales statement, but it's good. Often the hardest part of accomplishing anything is finding the time to do it. Maybe that's because we are always looking for time, trying to find time, or hoping for spare time when what we need to do is make time. I do realize that some things invade our life completely uninvited.

When I boarded an airplane in Springfield, MO bound for Indianapolis, IN and the engine blew up on take-off, my day was hit with a legitimate distraction. Was it scary? Yes. Even atheists were praying as we made the emergency landing with our heads between our knees, surrounded by fire trucks and ambulances on the runway. Distraction had definitely invaded my day. Flights were canceled. I had every reason to let that event circumvent my mission. The mission was to get to Indianapolis so I could speak to a group of people and help them become committed partners with a ministry.

Our days are invaded by phone calls that explode in our left ear, when in retrospect they're trivial by comparison to our main mission. We are distracted. We have itching ears to leave our main message. What did I do after the emergency landing? I jumped up and was first in line for a rebook on the next plane. I was informed the next plane would not get me to my event on time, so I called the rental car company and rented a car. I slipped the Delta agent a fifty-dollar bill to get my luggage off the plane. I got in the rental car and drove eight long, grueling hours to that night's event. Why? Because my priority that day was to fundraise with a particular group. It was booked. Gloria, my events scheduler, had it in my Google calendar, and I had it on my paper calendar. Yes, I completed the task despite the fact that everything around me was trying to distract me. We raised a lot of money that night.

## Carpe Diem
## — Horace (23 BC)

You have to push off distractions of every type if you really want to raise money. You cannot wait for the donor to approach you any more than you can wait for a fish to jump onto your plate fully cooked. The successful fundraiser has a list of people they would like to connect with and actively pursues a connection with those people. The successful fundraiser also has a list of current donors and contacts them regularly. The successful fundraiser schedules unshakable/unbreakable time slots each week to do nothing but work their specific target list.

**Time management is an oxymoron. Time is beyond our control, and the clock keeps ticking regardless of how we lead our lives. Priority management is the answer to maximizing the time we have.**
**— John C. Maxwell**

I know that many of you wear many hats in your office—fundraising is just one of them. I will bet if you had a doctor's appointment for next Wednesday at eleven-thirty, it would be on your calendar. You would make that appointment. "Hey Bill, can we golf on Wednesday morning?" You would turn down that invite because you prioritized your health. Well then, prioritize the financial health of the organization you serve as well. Schedule time for fundraising. Some centers are failing financially because their leadership is distracted. Time waits for no man.

If you are not fully funded, and not funded for a comfortable longer-term outlook, you need to devote seventy-five percent or more of your calendar to achieving that. Keep Monday clear to do other work. Monday morning is a horrible time to make phone contacts. However, Monday night is one of the best evenings to do banquets, connection calls, or individual presentations. What night is less interfered with than Monday night? Look at my presentation schedule, and you will see that Monday and Tuesday nights are always full.

If I looked at your calendar, would I see that you had scheduled time to speak to people about money? Is the support of your organization being reduced to chance meetings and chance times? Few people love fundraising, but having it scheduled will help keep you on track to do your expected work for your organization.

**I like to fish. On occasion, I catch them. I do that when I know what is in the water and adjust my lure to the fish's preference.
You don't use worms to catch Wicked Tuna.
— Gordon Douglas**

What does this fundraising schedule look like? Certainly, there are times of writing material for newsletters, prayer, planning for future events, lunches and dinners, and a lot of calls and emails to connect with people.

Where do we find these people? Have you called every name in the Christian business directory? How many times? Have you personally talked to a leadership representative (not the pastor) from every church? The internet is a wealth of knowledge if you work a mouse. You must actively, daily, and systematically pursue new donors and develop under-performing donors.

**The secret of your success is determined by your daily agenda.**
**— John C. Maxwell**

Years ago, while working on a fundraising project for a Haitian mission organization, I experimented with a time-out gift presentation. I found that in times of financial worry, it's best to ask for a reoccurring gift that has a built-in ending time. So, I asked for a monthly gift with an ending date of one year from then. This presentation gave the donor the ability to join the project, along with seeing light at the end of the tunnel if things got financially problematic for them. This one year, time-out gift encourages those who might drop out early to stay the course for the whole year. "We only have to do this for three more months. We can finish that." Of course, most people continue their monthly gift for years to come. If they are connected to an automated check situation, they will most likely continue to give for the next six years.

As a former pastor, I want to give you some insight into connecting with pastors. You have to schedule meeting times with any targeted pastors at good pastoral times. Try to connect on Tuesday, Wednesday, or Thursday morning. Provide a free lunch, and your odds increase. Connect with pastors through influencers in the church that have authority and wealth. A disinterested pastor will become amazingly interested if his wealthiest parishioner thinks that your ministry is amazing. Influential people control much of his topic and political stance. I speak as a licensed and ordained minister who pastored for a number of years. Your strategy should be to enlist the influencer to influence the pastor, who will then influence the congregation. Outside of the affluent influencer, how can you bring the church secretary into your circle of supporters? That secretary or executive assistant is your second-best pastor connector. Let's be honest, even the dedicated pro-life pastors do little more than fill a table with the youth pastor and the choir director at your banquet. We reach out to pastors to get an inroad to their congregations. Most churches give you less per month than a good monthly donor.

With the statistics showing that one out of every six pastors has had part in an abortion—fifty percent of that group have never shared it—you can see why they fear getting involved in your pro-life work. Their open, honest testimony could get them fired.

**TAKEAWAY:**

If you don't schedule time to fundraise, you will not raise funds. You must determine what priority funding your organization has and prioritize the appropriate time to do that. Your scheduling needs to include diverse groups of people with different presentations. Apathy in effective fundraising is as ungodly as others' apathy in not supporting your work. You need to clean and prepare your calendar for it today. How about now?

# 7

## What Is Your Blood Type?

**There are different kinds of gifts, but the same Spirit distributes them. There are different kinds of service, but the same Lord. There are different kinds of working, but in all of them and in everyone, it is the same God at work.**
**— Apostle Paul**

I have heard it said, "God doesn't call the equipped. He equips the called." That sounds really good when I'm preaching a sermon and want to encourage everyone in the room. But get real. Have you ever met a person who really loved and wanted to be a singer, even committed their life to singing for God, but yet … (pragmatic pause) … just couldn't sing? It did not seem like God was in a hurry to give them that amazing vocal gift either. Have you met that person yet? With that in mind, does God always equip those who think they are called?

I wouldn't hire a pastor who didn't have the ability to preach, believing God would somehow miraculously inspire him each week. Would you trust an airplane mechanic who was not skilled at airplane repair but really believed God would inspire him to fix your jet engine and stood in faith? As the ability to carry a tune might be a good starting point for a professional singer, personality, tenacity, or guts may be an opening requirement to be a successful fundraiser whether you feel "called" or not.

**If you can motivate people to charge Hell with a water pistol ... you will make a great fundraiser.**
**— Paul Aldrich**

Did you ever take a DISC test or a core personality test of some sort? Some people are not cut out for the spotlight. If you are a hardcore introvert, you will most likely not be a great fundraiser. Then again, you will not be a great leader of a charitable organization either. There is a certain audacity, spirit, drama, charm, daring, and grit that is needed to lead an organization. There is an outgoing boldness required. There is some sort of built-in leadership DNA that people want to follow. Some have it. Some don't. Some have it to a greater degree than others. Some have learned to develop it. Rejoice. For many it can be developed.

Those of you who have met me might think me to be an extrovert. I certainly do appear that way most times of the day. If you met me on a travel day, I might not have on my name tag, and I might not be wearing a well-pressed suit, and I might not even be well shaved. But when I arrive to speak at your event, I work to personally greet every person in attendance. There may be 800 people in the room, but I am going to try and look every person in the eye at least once and thank them for being at the event— before I get up in front of them to speak.

During these table meetings, it's not important for me to let them know who I am. At banquets, they often think I'm a caterer. I am often asked to retrieve some more coffee, which I do with rapid pace. I enjoy seeing their faces when I take the stage and they realize they asked the guest speaker to get them coffee.

I want to connect with people. But it isn't because I love people. I'm actually a bit of an introvert. Nevertheless, my occupation as a fundraiser requires me to put my own introverted style on the back burner and become super eye-contact making, longer hand-shaking, fundraising man. Raising money requires those who can learn to get out into the crowd and shake it up a little. It requires a person who knows how to—and is willing to—force themselves and their organization to the forefront of the conversation.

Small talk doesn't come natural for me. Am I good at it? Yes, but that is a trained ability, not a natural one. On the larger scene, men generally don't like small talk. We want to communicate an important message or watch football. This is why our gathering places are filled with large screens that keep us from having to say, "How does that make you feel?" about anything. You might be rather impressed by my table talk ability, but if you knew my inside… I have to psych myself up one hundred nights a year to become that guy. I have to do it, and I have to do it in a way that doesn't make the people I'm meeting feel as if it's tough for me. I must make the table guests, who also might be struggling with small talk, feel comfortable and calm with the conversation.

It's always a joy to me to stick out my hand to some big, burly redneck guy. He is already uncomfortable coming to this "thing" his wife forced him to get shaved for. As I shake his hand, I can read his mind. He's thinking, "Please don't ask me to talk. I got nothing to say. Please just move along to the next person." I love to engage that guy in a conversation. If I can, I give myself extra points for the night.

Good preparation will make you excited to present, rather than anxious. Excited people perform at higher levels than anxious people. Use that excitement to drive your creative connectedness. Soon you will find yourself comfortable in any circumstance talking small (and large) with anyone, anywhere. If you have the gift, you can go far. If you don't have the gift, develop it before you take the show on the road. I'm told that the Introvert's Guide to Small Talk should be required reading for anyone wanting to converse more comfortably.

## TAKEAWAY:

You must learn to talk to strangers and make them feel comfortable in your doing so. I find that preparing a small, memorized script can give me the confidence to get in, express my message, and retreat to the next table with everyone smiling. I now have ten different table small-talk introductions I can use to place me in the face of every person every night. I also mix them up so I'm not doing the same greeting within earshot of the preceding table. Do some research and write your own. You need it for more than a banquet. You need a table talk for the person you're passing at a restaurant who happens to make eye contact with you. You need a friendly information-gathering introduction for every person you meet in a grocery line, buffet line, or waiting room.

Any presenter knows that advantage of stepping on the platform having already met the audience. Any presenter who is truly concerned with connecting at a high level with your audience will find a way to arrive early enough to speak personally to as many of your potential donors as possible. It's your guest speaker's job. Make sure they do their job.

**HIGHLY SUGGESTED ADDITIONAL EDUCATION:**
I want to suggest the SCORRE Conference (http://www.scorreconference.tv) as your one stop to learn to speak to any audience large or small. It will be a weekend that will transform your speaking. It might just transform your world, as it did mine over two decades ago.

# 8

## Dress for Financial Success

**Though I am free and belong to no one, I have made myself a slave to everyone, to win as many as possible. To the Jews I became like a Jew, to win the Jews. To those under the law I became like one under the law (though I myself am not under the law), so as to win those under the law. To those not having the law I became like one not having the law (though I am not free from God's law but am under Christ's law), so as to win those not having the law. To the weak I became weak, to win the weak. I have become all things to all people so that by all possible means I might save some.**
**— Apostle Paul**

John T. Molloy wrote the 1975 business best seller

entitled Dress for Success. It systematically

cataloged the effect of clothing on a person's success

in business and personal life. In 1977, he followed with The Women's Dress for Success Book. In his tests, respondents subconsciously judged the clothing of a potential employee to see if the person fit in with other employees. His discoveries are still included in books and articles today. You can dress for success or failure.

**Clothing may not make the man,**
**but it might determine the response to the man.**
**— Terica Williams**

Your doctor dresses for success. His white polyester lab coat tells you that he knows more about the human body that you do. His staff wears a pajama-like outfit called scrubs. Wearing these in a medical office gives that person control of the room. This is the reason that so many PRCs are dressing their staff and volunteers in scrubs. The wearing of the scrubs gives them an increased influence on their clients. This will be the norm for PRCs in ten years. According to my lawyer, there's no legal precedent for wearing scrubs. I do know that if I grabbed my heart and hit the floor in a room filled with people, we would immediately look to the person wearing a lab coat, scrubs, or solid-colored pajamas to take charge. They may only be a veterinary assistant, or maybe they are wearing green pajamas, but their voice would carry the weight of skilled surgeon because of their outfit.

When I was a young speaker, trying to make a living with my voice, a mentor said, "Mike, always dress one small step better than your audience. It will give you control of the room." After doing this for twenty-five years, I have to concur with his hypothesis. So, where does that leave us in this chapter on fundraising and wardrobe?

**First impressions matter. Experts say we size up new people in somewhere between thirty seconds and two minutes.**
**— Elliott Abrams**

My very brilliant wife helps me write these books by attaching little Post-It notes with her thoughts to the printed manuscript. Because of the nature of this subject, I have chosen to simply reprint the note she left attached to this page. And I completely concur with her statement.

Mike, don't laugh, but your readers could learn a lot from Hillary Clinton. No matter where she goes, she always looks businesslike. Her traditional business pant suits are iconic. Any organization's director needs to be in their authoritative dress in public, especially at official PRC events. No matter how formal or informal their banquet is, for them it should be respectable business attire. Keep the collar high. There is no place that one should wear anything remotely plunging. All females can be very jealous and wary of women around their husbands. It is an understandable protective response in today's environment. Leaders should wear clothing that says they are a business professional. Leaders should wear clothing that allows them to bend over, or for that matter have a conversation, without having to clasp your neckline. Millennials should cover up the tattoos and remove the nose and lip rings when speaking to older people. Unfortunately, body piercing can make them look too young to be trusted

with hundreds of thousands of dollars. Church people love to judge—don't let them judge negatively. The staunchest critic can become the most generous donor if the leaders make that donor feel confident in their ability. Any true zealots for the pro-life cause will put their personal style and wardrobe freedom aside for the sake of the ministry. I believe this should also go for the PRC staff and board at the public fundraising events. Centers are judged by the look of everyone who is identified as part of the organization.
— TW

Let me take on the men for a minute. We need to dress businesslike as well. Casual clothing can make many of the older generation believe that you aren't serious about your work. It goes for both groups. Does your outfit say you are about business, or does it say you're simply biding your time in the office until you can get to the golf course?

Your jewelry speaks volumes about your person. It's supposed to. What does yours say about you? Does it say you are super wealthy? Does it say you are flashy? Some churches frown on large or attractive jewelry. Call it stupid, but they felt that way all through Bible times. Our freedom has to be in check according to our audience, and your audience is usually conservative.

In fifteen years, some of these dress concerns won't be an issue, but they are today. Get over it. Do what you have to do to get the job done. Nobody considers our military to be sell-outs or compromisers for wearing sand-colored camouflage outfits when fighting in desert locations. It's not what they wear at home with their wife and children. Tacticians understand the surroundings. It's called wisdom. Think about it.

As I sat with a post-abortion counselor this last week, she made an interesting statement. "I personally hate those little golden feet pins used to remind people of the feet of an aborted baby. They bring up bad memories for the one out of every three women in our country who have had an abortion. I have yet to hear of one woman who was headed for an abortion and saw a fifty-year-old man in a line at the grocery store wearing a golden feet pin and changed her mind about the abortion." This counselor made a good point. Would you wear a little golden flame while you were in a group of people to remind others how their family members who don't know God are going to hell? Why not? Maybe we should get little golden cigarettes on a black tombstone to expose the dangers of smoking. Golden syringes could bring awareness of the heroin epidemic. You are in the fundraising and life-saving business. Why would you risk offending the people who you are about to ask for support? Love your donors and be respectful of their emotions. Many pro-life donors are those who previously had an abortion. This was not the first time I heard this no-feet-pins concept. I have had ladies tell me how hurtful those little pins are many times before.

Match your business clothing to the financial level of your donor. Don't pull up to a mobile home in a car that costs more than the mobile home. Don't meet a businessperson in cut-offs and flip flops. Don't wear a golden-feet pin through your nose or your lapel.

## TAKEAWAY:

Your dress will determine how quickly you are welcomed into the heart and confidence of a donor. Dress for the occasion. While we aren't advocating an Amish wardrobe, we do encourage you and your team to dress in a way that will install confidence in your organization and eliminate the possibility of judgment from your audience. Always wander toward the side of conservative.

# 9

## Curiosity Kills Cats

**Whoever has ears to hear, let them hear.
— Jesus Christ**

Last year, I raised a few thousand dollars for my mission by just taking a nap with a photo book. I fly an average of two hundred flights a year. That means that two hundred times a year, I'm sitting next to a stranger. I love to get out my little picture book. It contains some really interesting, even gut-wrenching photos. I lay it open on my tray table, lean back, and take a nap. When I wake from turbulence or a crying baby, I turn to another page and go back to napping. Curiosity kills the cat, and photos attract neighboring eyes.

Toward the end of the flight, the pilot will announce for us to prepare for landing. At this time, I sit up and move the photos to the armrest between myself and the neighboring flyer. I give them every opportunity to ask me what the photos are about. Often they do. I respond with my best ninety-second pitch. The rest is a matter of sending thank you notes. I have one fellow who's consistently given one thousand dollars every year for multiple years after such a photo nap. I don't suggest that you take flights with photos as an effective way for you to fund your organization, but I do believe in the power of pictures.

**You push the button, we do the rest. Light makes photography. Embrace light. Admire it. Love it. But above all, know light. Know it for all you are worth, and you will know the key to photography. — George Eastman**

Sometimes when I'm going to personally share with someone, I'll first take out a very nice jewelry box and hold it in my hand. I'll prep my listener by saying, "I want to show you something amazing, but before I do, let me tell you a story…" I then launch into my short fundraising pitch while holding the jewelry box in front of me. In the box is a picture of a child. Most of the time, I never open the box. If I'm good, my story is going to supersede their interest in the box. The box is just there to hold attention until my story has captivated their mind.

A picture is worth a thousand words, and a picture with a well-honed fifty-word narrative is worth a thousand dollars. Welcome to the digital age. Most of us have a camera on our phone that rivals the best Minoltas and Canons of twenty years ago. Those cameras can also hold a file of every photo we could ever want to use to illustrate a point. Nevertheless, a good 8X10 is really hard to beat. You can use a picture to be your jewelry box distracter.

**Photography takes an instant out of time, altering life by holding it still.**
**— Dorothea Lange**

Jesus used parables to draw vivid images in minds. He also used graphic illustrations, putting spit and mud in eyes, writing names in the sand, and cursing olive trees. The earlier churches learned to teach through pictures that were constantly before the people and illuminated by the sunlight through the stained glass.

When I'm making a presentation about our mission work, I love to have one good picture in my hand. I wave it around a little to peak their interest. I don't want the picture to distract from my presentation. I might let them look at the picture momentarily and then take it back, face it toward me, and present my ninety seconds of why before I put the photo in their hand again. This keeps their conversation on the theme at hand. Distractions are the devil's scheme.

### The soul never thinks without a picture.
### — Aristotle

Visual aids, such as pictures, can be great conversation pieces. One might be a picture of a child eating a purple cupcake or riding in a wagon. Does the picture interest those who see it? That is the picture you're looking for. It might be something less photographic, yet illustrative in nature. Maybe it's a quilt that was made by a client or a letter with a crayon drawing from a child who was rescued by your organization. Ask God for creativity and get creative.

**This amazing crayon drawing was made possible by the people in this room that rescued the unborn artist from an abortion three years ago.
— A PRC Director**

I want to talk to you about what I call charitable racism. Let's be real honest. We live in a world where people have pre-disposed feelings about religious, political, and even racial groups. Don't fight that battle. Your job is not to fight the racial battle. Your job is to support life-saving work by raising funds. If you turn down every dollar that comes from someone with a racial, political, spiritual, or philosophical difference, you will only need a small piggy bank. Carry multiple pictures of children of different ethnicities. Use photos that correspond to the same race of the person you are speaking to. This goes for all the races, for racism comes in all colors. Show that your organization is serving "their" people, and not just the Spanish-speaking migrant worker or the single black mother or the wealthy white girl from the suburbs. Show a white donor a white-faced child, a black donor a black-faced child, a Hispanic donor a Hispanic-faced child, and so on. Some people are appalled when I talk about this, but those people aren't aware of how racial demographics play into every advertisement they see on television.

Some of you need a minute to take in that last paragraph. Fine. Take a few breaths, get a coffee. The truth is ugly and often hurts. Fundraising is a tough, full-contact sport, so wear a helmet. If I'm not honest with you, this book will have failed before it even started.

I have made many presentations in houses, seated on a couch in the living room. If the television is on, even if the sound is off and only the screen is active, I say, "I am ADD. Would you mind if I turned the television off? I want to be able to give you the full attention you deserve." Then I reach down and hit the off button on their remote, as if they have given me that permission. You are in charge of making sure the listener is set up to listen to your presentation. Find the right times and give them a visual alternative to keep their mind's eye attracted.

Sometimes when I go into an office to meet with a businessman, as the secretary opens the door and performs the expected introductions, I jokingly say, "Carol, please hold any calls that come in for me. I want to be able to give Mr. Smith my undivided attention for five full minutes." Then I laugh and pull out my 8X10 picture or my jewelry box. It's time to raise some money.

If you have ever met me at a conference, you know that I get right to the point. Some exhibitors say, "Please take any information you want" as their table is full of different brochures and candy. My table is not. I often sit halfway out in the middle of the aisle. When you pass me, I place a book (the visual picture) in your hand as I launch into a fundraising conversation:

"I need forty-five seconds of your time. Question. Did your last banquet net you four hundred dollars for every person who was in your room?" (I will do the math for them on their banquet.) "It breaks my heart when PRCs aren't receiving the funding they can receive. Other centers are averaging those financial numbers in similar neighborhoods.

"I'm sorry, I get ahead of myself. Let me introduce myself. I can't do this in the humble manner I would like to in ninety seconds, so forgive me. Here goes. My name is Mike G. Williams, I have been the most booked and re-booked PRC fundraising speaker in the country for the past fourteen years. I like the rebooked part best, as anybody can get booked. But when was the last time you booked a speaker five times in a row? I have been blessed. I have also been the top multi-million-dollar Ambassador Agency fundraiser for PRCs for the past ten years.

"Question. Are you choosing your presenter based on a good story or their ability to make money for your organization? I have a great testimony of my rescue adoption and the rescue-adoption of my son, but what is important is my ability to raise a lot of money in a way that makes people happy. A way that makes them want to come back the next year. I want to raise a lot of money for you.

"Three questions. When is your next banquet? Do you want to raise more money than past years? And what questions can I answer for you to get my name on your most successful fundraising event ever?"

Did it take me more than forty-five seconds? Who cares, really? If this is information that is going to make you money, we all have time. I have your attention with the book in your hand and another book and clipboard in my hand. You may wonder if my presentation works. Well, you might want to remember that I have been the most booked and re-booked speaker for the past fourteen years. So yes, it works, and so do my presentations at those events.

For PRCs, there's nothing better than a happy child picture to keep the attention of the listener and reinforce the message of your life saving work.

## TAKEAWAY:

The picture you use will become the poster child for whatever your ninety-second pitch is. Make it a superlative demographic-matching picture. You can make a presentation without a picture, but when you have time to prepare, don't leave home without it. Use the picture to distract the possible donor from their surroundings and keep them focused on your message. Keep the focus as Jesus did.

# 10

## Prepare to Receive

**When those around balked and rejected His first healing declaration to the crippled man, Jesus went with another option saying,
"Rise up and walk."
— St. Mark**

Air Force One is one of the most sophisticated planes in the air. It has everything, including the ability to refuel while in flight. There is a port on top of the fuselage that allows a hose to be extended from a fuel tanker plane and connect in-flight to supply the fuel needed. Do you think it's important for both planes to have the same type and size of connector? Was it a good idea to have worked out this operation on the ground before they were dealing with a critical airborne fueling situation?

**There will be time enough for counting, when the dealing's done.**
**— Kenny Rogers**

There may be a tendency for many of you to skip this chapter. You may be thinking it's only about banquets, or you're believing you have a good response mechanism already in place. Please hear me out.

I arrived early to the fundraising banquet, as I always do. There is a lot a speaker needs to do to prepare to be the best for the client. In that time, I met with the banquet planner and went over the needs of the center and exactly how much they wanted to use as a monthly donation target number for the audience. I always go over the response card and make sure I know it well. I said, "Could I have a copy of your response card?" A blank look came over her face. "Ah … we just thought that people would go home tonight and send us their donations next week. Ah … I guess we could get some buckets and pass them around." I accidentally laughed out loud. Needless to say, that center got exactly what they had prepared to receive. I'm told that leader is no longer at that center.

I see wonderful organizations every week who fail miserably in their ability to receive funds. Often their financial response cards are a tragedy. If the receiving plane doesn't have the same connecting device as the supply plane, the receiving plane will run out of gas and crash.

**At that time the kingdom of heaven will be like ten virgins who took their lamps and went out to meet the bridegroom. Five of them were foolish and five were wise. The foolish ones took their lamps but did not take any oil with them. The wise ones, however, took oil in jars along with their lamps.**
**— Jesus Christ**

People are fickle. Why would any forward-thinking board or director have limited financial receptacle tubing connected to their organization? We live in a world where a large giving demographic is infatuated with getting airplane bonus miles by using their credit cards. They want to use everything to help bring about that "free travel".

**The horrible secret is that many a donation isn't just about you.**
**— Justin Fennell**

You may have made the greatest pitch of your life to three hundred people. Do you have multiple methods for them to respond? Will you make them all wait in lines as amateurs nervously try to process that information on an iPhone using a little plastic plug-in device? Though having a square micro terminal is excellent—and you should have one with you at all times—it is often the apex of small thinking when you plan to use one at a large event. Small thinking continues in not having a way to establish a reoccurring, monthly, automated check system. Most any bank can set this up for you. Your organization should be prepared to take credit cards, checks, stock donations, property donations, and cash, though cash is the last thing you should be attempting to receive.

**Automated check donors will stay with your organization an average of six-plus years. This is not rocket science. It is, however, fundraising science. Credit cards change and get cancelled, but people stay with their bank. Checking accounts don't have an expiration date.**
**— George Eusterman, creator of E-Giving**

While driving to an event in Middle America, I couldn't help but notice the many farms with many barns. The open barns revealed many years of tractors lined up inside. Understanding the financial plight of the American farmer, and thinking that this could be a possible unique revenue stream for my client, that night I asked for people with an extra tractor to donate it to the center. I guess I presented it in a way that sold them on the idea. "I would rather stand before God having saved the lives of children than telling Him I had three valuable tractors in my barn rusting away," was my additional message. We received two tractors that night and turned them into twenty-five thousand dollars in additional revenue for the center. I don't believe your financial response cards should include a box for used tractors, unless you work in one of those areas.

When you give an ask, have as many methods of receiving your fuel as possible. Don't confess you're ready for a banquet, unless you are ready— fully ready—to receive from all angles. Some say that in their area, people don't give electronically. Well, times are changing. The Millennials don't know any other way. Prepare for the future or be stuck in the past.

When you are presenting to one person or one couple, it's a little uncomfortable to pull out a response card and ask them to fill it out while you play soft, reverent music on your iPhone. So just ask. ASK. "What is the best way for you to complete your desire to solve this problem?" If the donor says they would like to send a check, give them your card and circle the name the check should be made out to and underline the proper address. Follow up by sending them a thank you note the next day, even before you receive the gift. Keep feet from cooling by moving those feet in a forward manner. You might return a note that offers your appreciation for their desire to be part of the solution. Always go back to your why story in that correspondence. You could include a self-addressed, stamped envelope as a courtesy. Always mention that you will call them in a few days to again say thank you and to let them know that your organization has received the gift so they won't worry about that.

## TAKEAWAY:

Prepare to receive from your donor through your donor's easiest portal. Move all reoccurring (monthly) donors to automated checks if possible. Be as prepared to receive a gift as you are to ask for the gift. Never drop the financial ball on the one-yard line.

# 11

## The Dance of the Steward

**As a result of your ministry they will give glory to God. For your generosity to them and to all believers will prove that you are obedient to the good news of Christ.**
**— Apostle Paul**

In this chapter, I hope to implant two axioms into your minds. The first is that we must teach stewardship in our newsletters and correspondence with our donors. We must do it in an altruistic way. In raising our donor's stewardship intellect, they will more cheerfully give to our work and the work of others. Secondly, we need to model stewardship in our own organization.

**Fundraising is the gentle art of teaching the joy of giving.**
**— Henry Rosso**

Maybe, just maybe, the teachings on stewardship currently on display are all wrong. They fall into a number of categories. You have the "Give to us and God will give back to you one hundred fold" believers. It's hard to compete with a promise like that. I'm not saying that God won't bless your giving, but I personally don't like to make promises for God. I might overstate His desired blessing, or I might limit it by my thinking. There's the general message of the modern church: "Give us your ten percent as the Bible said was the correct amount, and then give us offerings above that for special things that we want to support, but not from our general budget." By the way, "general budget" is not a term found in the Bible. Some would argue the modern church has gotten away from the proper use of the tithe (being about feeding the poor and so on as found in Matthew 25) and moved to using the money to create a bit of a social club for those with similar beliefs. One cannot step into a mega-church building, often half full, used only one day a week, and not ask if the money could have been better used to feed the world rather than host concerts once a month. But hey, I'm sure God likes flashing lights and fog as much as the next guy. In between those two points, there are a lot more variations on the giving theme.

Use your newsletter to promote the blessings of giving to your ministry. Share testimonies of givers, not just rescued children and needs. We will discuss how to do this in later chapters, but use the peer pressure of donor testimonies to drive your monthly gifts.

The donor who shares how they gave in the midst of a personal hard time and was blessed through it will encourage others to continue to give through hard times. Our newsletters are going to donors, so speak messages to donors.

**Cast your bread upon the water and it will come back to you pressed down, shaken together, and running over.**
**— Jesus Christ**

Nevertheless, if the great mission promise of Jesus (Acts 1:8) is to be believed, then maybe our giving—which includes that going to a local church—should be divided into four quadrants. A fourth goes to the local ministry (Jerusalem), a fourth to closer work but not us (Judea), a fourth to a special needs or disenfranchised group (Samaria), and a fourth to support a foreign work (the uttermost parts of the world). Of course, you might not want to rock the standard giving world's norm, even if you are correct. That is a way to get yourself beheaded by the most loving Christian pastors in the world. The business part of the church will decapitate you quickly if you start messing with the money. But let's find ways to teach that as stewards, we are responsible for where our money is used. This means that we should sit as watchdogs over the spending trends of our churches and parachurch groups. We need to hold them accountable to use the tithes and offerings for true God works.

**Those who live by the sword shall die by the sword.**
**— Aeschylus's Agamemnon, 458 B.C.**

It's time for the second axiom I want to drag into this chapter. I learned the word reciprocal many years ago. It's a good word, a wise word, a true word. What you plant you receive. What you give, you get. You, as an organization who receives from others' giving, need to be generous in our support of others. If God can expect a portion of the money He provides a person to be returned in giving, then an organization can naturally be expected to give back to Him by giving to another work. Does that need to be a tenth? I don't know. I do know the organizations that are blessed are those who also give back to others.

**No one has ever become poor by giving.**
**— Anne Frank**

What upcoming mission work does your organization support? Are you supporting a similar work in some other part of the world? I hear PRCs constantly talking about the millions of children aborted, when they are only working in a local demographic. Maybe we need to broaden our scope. Why not support a third-world center? In doing so, we know that God will bless us. In doing so, we can truly speak to our donors and tell them of the global influence they are having. In accounting, you will find that it costs little or nothing to support third-world works.

**How can any organization, in good conscience, receive a share of what others are given and not find a place in which to give to the next generation of needs themselves? That kind of greed is scary. I would not want to be on that board on the judgment day.**
**— Brian White**

I think my ministry and yours needs to ask some genuine questions. Is our ministry one sided? Are we any different than the churches who don't support us? Does your PRC receive money from other ministries or churches that are sharing a portion of their gifts with you? Of course you do. We expect it. We grumble if churches don't support our work. We often call them greedy or self-serving. Listen, if we are going to survive by the generous stewardship of others, then we need to model it ourselves. I personally am not going to give you a dime until I know what you are doing with it. I want to also know that you are building forward for the cause. The non-religious world calls it paying it forward. Let's at least meet their secular standards.

### Be the donor you want to have.
### — Terica L. Williams

For sake of full disclosure, please know that my wife and I started a third-world mission and subsequently helped develop two third-world PRCs. I have a vested interest in this matter. In relationship to these centers, I have asked numerous PRCs how they were partnering with other centers in the third world. I found that few would get involved because they see their own organization as a receiving-only organization. Some of them don't see themselves as financially solvent enough to help others. I believe that our financial solvency comes when we are reciprocally blessed by God.

Being true to my own fundraising teaching, I would remind you to start your support for a third world PRC today at www.CupsOfColdWater.com where we will transform the life of a pregnant girl and her baby through life skills education and medical support. Could I ask for one penny out of each of your donated dollars to rescue eighty-five girls every week? One little penny out of every dollar will allow you to share your international impact with your donors, claiming eighty-five lives are being transformed in the Dominican Republic every week of every year as an extension of your organization.

## TAKEAWAY:

We need to use the voice and relationship we have with our partners/donors to teach true stewardship in our newsletter correspondence. If we rely on others to teach it, it won't happen. Understanding that we all receive commensurately to that which we have given, we must find organizations of like mission and support their work. To not give vigorously to others is to put a cork in our own bottle of supply.

# 12

## Repetition Is More Than the Best Teacher

**Go and make disciples…**
**— Jesus Christ**

I hear it said, "We just need to get some new donors to come to the event." I agree if you have done a bad job of developing your old ones. Look at the facts. New givers are what we call tire kickers in professional fundraising circles. They give a little and want to see the results before they give you anything substantial.

New givers are great. We love them. We want them. We look for them. But their dollar-giving potential will increase when they become repeated, discipled, developed givers. First gifts are based on your presentation, as seen in previous chapters. Larger follow-up gifts are based on our newest, captivating presentations and the donor's great past experience with us. You have proved your expertise in meeting the goals of the previous project. Little gifts generate better gifts, which generate even better gifts.

**Donor loyalty is not about the donor being loyal to you, it is you being loyal to the donor.**
**— Harvey McKinnon**

Repeat givers cost you less to engage. They're already aware of you. You know them. You already have their credit card numbers. The trust factor is already in place. When we take repeat donors for granted, we make a big mistake. When we look to new donors to be the big windfall for our needs, we make a big mistake.

We teach our children to change the oil on the car, change the filter on the air conditioner, change the filter on the water purifier. We teach them that maintenance is needed and necessary for financial success. The cost of maintaining a car is much less than buying a new one. The cost of maintaining a home A/C system is less than buying a new one. In fact, now might be a good time to change those filters, while you're thinking about it. Treat your donors the same way; service them.

**Retention is the new acquisition.**
**Customer service is the new marketing.**
**— Joe Connelly**

Stop looking for new money until you have gotten all the money out of the old pants. Develop, develop, develop your current friends. Your donors are your friends. They are possibly better friends than those you play UNO with on Saturday night. These are friends that truly share their wallet with you.

I have a pastor in a foreign country who calls me every two weeks. He calls until he gets me. No voice mail. No email. No texting. A real, live conversation. He calls not to ask for money, but rather to find out how my family is and how he can pray for us. He could be making random calls to strangers—new donor development—asking for money, but he chooses to call me every two weeks to ask about my family. Sometimes when he calls, I notice a bit of sadness in his voice. I ask how I can be of help. Seeing that I am here and he is there, help usually involves a check and a Western Union office. Because of his faithfulness to care about me, I naturally want to care about him. It is me who usually engages the "how can I help" question. That's the kind of financial partner you want. His relationship development with me and my family has won him thousands of dollars over the years, and we give it not begrudgingly, but as a friend.

## TAKEAWAY:

Work as hard on the development of relationships with the current financial partners as you do in finding new ones. You're more likely to see efficient increase from the repetitive sector. There's a reason Jesus chose to make disciples rather than constantly look for new converts. That is what He taught us to do.

# 13

## Financial Competition, Organizational Leeches, and Politicians

**You will not associate with these peoples left among you or speak the names of their gods. — Joshua**

I'm going to keep this simple. Our financial competition is not UnPlanned Parenthood, Sex Ed Teachers Association of North America, Condom Distributors of Texas, Pro-Abortion Advocates of California, or any other irreligious group on the scene with a website and a Washington lobby. They are definitely an adversary to our public message but not an adversary to our funding.

One PRC has used me many times at their banquet. Each time they remind me, "Don't say anything negative about Planned Parenthood, as one of their local leaders attends our banquet every year and supports us financially." Some of you are turning flips thinking of taking money from a PP person. Because of their choice, this very effective PRC has learned to fight for good without having to anger the bad. Whose story are you telling, their victory and our defeat, or your victory? Should I tell you about the PRC that became friends with the PP staff to the extent that when the PP closed, they donated their ultrasound machine to the PRC?

Keep your events and presentations about your work, your accomplishments, and your rescues. People are aware of what the others are doing, so they need no advertising at your events. Your enemy is not the Democratic party any more than it is the Republican party. Neither party is going to change anything. There is too much money involved. The Republicans count the cost of 42 million more Democrats living and voting against them if abortion rights were overturned. The Democrats count the cost of maintaining 42 million more people on welfare. Don't get involved in the great political misdirection. Stay with the plan. Rescue children and transform families.

Your financial competition comes from every other parachurch group or semi-religious charity in your area who is seeking to tap deeply into the limited resources of the good, moral, and decent people of your community. You need to love them, all the while winning the financial race for your charity. If you don't think you deserve to win that race, you need to be ethical enough to leave your group and go join the charity you believe does.

Quietly attend the fundraising events of the other players in your area. You should know who they are, what they're doing, and how they're doing it. You might even meet some people who would also be interested in helping you. Almost every night there is another organization represented at the fundraising banquets I speak at. Why? They're smart. They often figure out a way to be recognized from the platform.

Wow. Why aren't you doing that at other banquets? Better yet, why are you acknowledging these groups at yours? Does McDonald's give a shout out to the Burger King next door and tell you how well they produce the Whopper? No.

**Everything I know about politics, my Dad taught me when I was about ten years old. He said, "Son, politics is taken from two words: Poly, which means many, and Ticks, which are blood-sucking creatures." Time has proven Dad to be a wise man.**
**— Gordon Douglas**

I know that you believe in your politicians, and I know they have done amazing work in stopping or limiting abortion in your state (hopefully), but let them receive the glory for their accomplishments at their own banquet. See if they are really on your side. Invite them to come, but tell them you cannot recognize them from the stage. I'll bet their presence might somehow have to be rescheduled.

Feature your work in your presentations. If you are a start-up, then sell what you would like to do with the money you will receive. I remember well the night the politician took the stage for his scheduled ninety-second spot. He pulled out a plaque to award to another politician in the room for his pro-life stance. That politician then came to the platform to accept his award and pulled out another plaque to give to another politician in the room. That awarded politician in the room then proceeded to the platform to remind everyone to vote for all three of them in the upcoming election. About seven minutes into this trade, I whispered in the ear of the guy on my left, who happened to be Ryan Dobson. "What would your dad do right now?" Ryan quietly explained that his dad would have never let it get to this point to begin with.

## TAKEAWAY:

Keep your presentation focused on your success, the current need, and how the people in front of you can meet that need for X-amounts of dollars. Everything else—special music, slide shows of volunteers, political guests, political rantings, and coffee refills—are just distractions from what you are trying to do at a financial presentation or public fundraiser, which is to raise funds.

# 14

## Never Book a Guest Speaker

**A prophet is often without honor in his own country.**
**— Jesus Christ**

There are a lot of organizations who do a great job of raising their own money, in-house, with their own staff providing all the presentation. It can be done. People are doing it. Celebrate. But before you jump into this endeavor, prove yourself to yourself and to your board. What is your success rate on personal fundraising endeavors? It takes a lot more skill and timing to connect with two hundred people at one time than it does to connect with two. Make sure you're doing really well with your individual lunch appointment presentations, and then begin to script a larger version of that same, well-working SIX-R presentation. Eliminate anything in the program that does not tie directly to the needs of your donors, and share your heart out. Your goal should be to receive an average of four hundred dollars or more per person. Our stats have shown that when you are receiving this four-hundred-dollar number (fifteen percent more in the oil and gas belt) from every individual person between the ages of twenty-five and sixty-five at your event, you are operating at very close to optimal average for a banquet event. When you can receive that on your own, stop paying for a speaker, and do your own everything.

Let's be honest. There are very few guest speakers that can really attract new people to your work. There are speakers who can draw a crowd, but their ability to motivate those people to join you are most often overshadowed by their own star persona. Don't get your hopes up if you bring in a national celebrity speaker. They will most likely do the same or less than a really good, lesser-known, lesser paid speaker. I could tell you horror stories about big-name guest speakers who drove the event cost through the ceiling, and their audience walked out as soon as they were done speaking. Don't let the booking agents lead you astray. The people in your audience will be there mostly because of you and your table hosts' encouragement to come. A celebrity speaker may help your attendance a little, but unless the celebrity is willing and able to turn their fans into your donors, the celebrity will benefit you none. They may even be a distraction from your work. I can tell you some horror stories along that illustrative line.

Never book a guest speaker thinking they are going to be the end-all answer to your budget needs. A great speaker can and should help you achieve the best result, but often the result is less than what could have been because the organization didn't set up the speaker to do their best. If the set-up is bad, Jesus Himself might not be able to get people to give sacrificially to you. Large group, event fundraising is a team sport.

Think of a guest fundraising speaker as an effective clean-up batter. If you load the bases, that speaker will drive everyone on base to home plate. You must make sure you've loaded the bases. Prepare your guest speaker to succeed for you by creating an event that mirrors a fundraising talk. The entire event should bring passionate, captivating illustrations of why you do what you do and the success you've had. Your speaker will reinforce that and then ask them to pay the bill for it to continue. Set your speaker up to hit, what they call in baseball, a four-run home run. Load your bases and get ready for the professional pitch. I have made my living since 2002 being a clean-up batter. My agent uses my track record as the most booked speaker and immediately re-booked speaker as a selling point. I guess people don't repeat something that didn't do very well. But remember, you can get good enough to do your own ask.

Never choose a guest speaker for your fundraising event based on anything other than their proven track record to raise large numbers of funds, as you are doing a fundraiser, not hosting a story time. This is where so many groups fail in their speaker choice. Somebody hears a good story and says, "Let's have them come and tell that interesting story to our group and ask for money." Well, Goldilocks and the Three Bears is a heartwarming story, but if it isn't connected directly with what your organization does, then it's just a story about bears and will bring you no added dollar value. Stop booking fundraising speakers because they have a good story.

Let me give you a simple way to pick your next fundraising speaker. Get your potential speakers' phone numbers. Call the speakers you are considering and interview them on the phone. Ask them to tell you in 90 seconds why they would be your best fundraiser. If they can't meet the criteria for a successful pitch for themselves, what do you think they can do for you? Secondly, ask them to articulate how they would do their financial ask for you. Can they do it and leave you wanting to give over the phone? Celebrity status means nothing if that celebrity cannot produce for you. You are having a fundraising event, not an autograph time. Beware of board members who subconsciously desire to bring in a celebrity they are enamored with.

It's been my experience that athletes often have the worst record for fundraising events, followed closely by singers. Fundraising is rarely in a musical or athletic professional's skill set. Be aware of that now, before you book your next fundraiser. Be careful of the former quarterback-turned-gospel-singer who also does fundraising events twice a year. Just because someone can catch a football does not mean they can catch thousands of dollars for you. When you do your requested phone interview, this should be obvious. A bad speaker will have his or her agent protect them from such interviews for this reason. They will call it privacy or tell you the speaker is too busy to call you before the event is contracted. Laugh and hang up the phone.

I remember the night a famous athlete finished his talk about his career in the NFL. Certainly, he was going to talk about his belief in the pro-life movement and his support for the local work next, as this was a pregnancy resource center banquet. No, he didn't. He must have been hit on the head too many times to remember why he was there. He asked if anyone had any questions and sat down, leaving the director to scramble and figure out how to close the very banquet that she hired the gridiron pro to close. Don't let a board member who wants to cozy up to his childhood athletic hero or camouflage-wearing reality show stars determine the outcome of your fundraiser, even if they are paying the contract.

No matter who your speaker is, you need their personal phone number. You are hiring a speaker, not their agent.

You have to do the math too! If your in-house leader can bring you ten thousand dollars for free, and a hired gun can bring you fifty thousand dollars for a cost of five thousand in fees, you would have to be ignorant not to use a professional. Let me give you a few tips on making your professional speaker experience less costly.

## GUEST SPEAKER PREPARATORY AND MONEY-SAVING NOTES
(I know the agents are going to hate me for this.)

1. Sometimes a speaker is asking a lot more than you have ever paid before. Ask the speaker to put their money where their mouth is. If they are that good at raising money, they can share the risk. Offer them a reasonable fee for their services connected with a percentage bonus for any amount they bring in above what your best speaker did in previous years. If they are good enough, this won't scare them a bit. This will separate the genuine professional sheep from the amateur goats. If they perform up to what they promise, they get rewarded. If their promo is all hype, then they get a fee worthy of their performance.

2. Never ask how much a speaker charges. Instead, submit an offer. Often, the speaker will accept an offer if they see it in front of them. If the agent says they won't accept it, tell them to submit it

anyway. Include a letter as to why you deserve a special price. See if your wonderful speaker has any compassion in their heart too. Fees are always negotiable. Negotiate vigorously. If they can't sell you on why they are worth the money in that phone interview, I will bet they can't sell your organization either. If your preferred speaker will not negotiate your rate, negotiate the sliding pay scale noted in the first point. You could offer a higher dollar amount than the speaker is asking for if they can hit your large targeted goal.

3.  Look for hidden fees in the contract. Does your speaker need special sound or video requirements that are going to cost you additional money? Negotiate for the speaker to pay for a portion of their needed production. A hotel will charge outrageous amounts for the smallest of items. Be aware of hidden fees.

4.  Offer the speaker a reasonable flat fee for travel. This means that you don't have to deal with paperwork and receipts that follow. Negotiate what you think is a good flat rate and make the

speaker responsible for getting to you, covering their own plane ticket, rental car, even hotel. Remove some of the details from your hand.

5.   Hire the speaker for the entire day. This means that you can use them to speak multiple times for you in one day. You may choose to add a senior luncheon to your banquet schedule, and they can speak for that too. Agents love to add money, but speakers love to speak. Make sure you own them for the day. Don't ask your speaker what they want for a schedule, give them the one you want. You are the client, not the indentured servant. By treating guest speakers like prima donnas, we have created the diva attitudes and rock star prices we see today. Stop it. Would Jesus have needed all of this?

6.   Require your chosen speaker to arrive in the morning, giving you a fallback flight if the original one cancels for any reason. When they do arrive early, they can visit your center to see what they are raising money for. Any speaker who doesn't want to know you shouldn't speak for you.

7. Give your speaker a list of your expectations. Mine would include arriving before doors open at the event and personally greeting everyone coming through the doors or going from table to table during the dinner to meet the people. This is something that sets you up for a win. Every board member should be doing this as well.

8. Provide your speaker with a list of needs and their corresponding dollar amounts. People give to specific projects more enthusiastically than to ambiguous general offerings. Include yearly/monthly cost of earn/learn material, operation of ultrasound, rent, electricity, pregnancy tests, STI tests, abstinence program material, and training. Get creative with multiple buy-in amounts. You need large gift points and lower gift points.

9. Require a phone number and a phone interview with the speaker before you sign the contract, not after. If they can't talk to you now, they won't communicate after you have signed a contract.

10. Make sure the agency booking your speaker has a large enough roster to provide you with another speaker in the case of a medical emergency. Don't be caught holding the bag when your speaker gets ill or decides another event would be better for their career. It does happen. Don't pay that replacement the same amount of the original contract. Demand the same kind of contractual respect the agency wants from you.

11. Never use an internet company to book a hotel room. Always deal directly with the local hotel and arrange for an early check-in. If there's a problem or a last-minute change, the ten dollars you saved booking online will be met with a lot of sorrow for you and the guest coming. Any good speaker has a hotel they prefer to work with. Ask them for their preferences. It means a lot to a person on the road all the time to have the same type of bed to sleep in.

12. Some organizations ask the speaker to give back a portion of their income to the organization in the form of a check. Consider the impact on an

audience when a speaker says, "I believe so much in this organization that I, too, am writing a check tonight, right along with you."

## TAKEAWAY:

Until you are ready to completely do your own events, including the ask, choose your speaker from their proven financial success track record, not their celebrity status. Set up your speaker to bring in great financial numbers by creating an event that speaks to the heart and calls for action. Your event needs to do on a large scale what a personal funding presentation does on a personal level. When you become very successful at your small group presentations, give it a go at your own banquet. Maybe the board could, as a bonus, give you the fee they would normally pay that speaker. Just a suggestion.

# 15

## Raising Money with Food

### We only have five loaves and two fishes.
### — St. Mark

The most effective way to articulate our deepest
thoughts are over a good meal. The ministry of Jesus
seems to be summed up when He sits at the table
and shares with the disciples. Humorously, I might
remind you that this was also where they all moved to
one side of the table for a group photograph. Food is
where it's at. I've seen groups who've tried to move
people to give large amounts of money in concert
seating situations. I've been brought in to do the
professional ask at these events, and I have rarely

seen a concert seating situation deliver what a sit-down dinner does. Food is the gateway to the wallet and the purse. This includes one-to-one fundraising presentations.

### Spaghetti dinners bring spaghetti dollars.
### — Gordon Douglas

I love that line, and Gordon Douglas knows. He has been delivering top fundraising numbers for many, many years. The truth is that unless you're in a totally blue-collar area, stay away from cheap dinners. If you're going to invest in a banquet, get the food right, and serve it quickly. Don't do anything other than offer a short prayer of thanksgiving—not a sermon on the pro-life stance of God—before your audience is eating. People don't remember anything before they eat, so why would we want to present anything before they eat? Be wise!

Great fundraising has as much to do with food delivery time as it does the pitch. Give them a great meal served quickly. Have your quality, including the temperature of the food and delivery times, guaranteed in writing by the caterer. A real guarantee has a financial penalty for failure to deliver.

**Isaac negotiated the birthright from his brother with the promise and delivery of a really good soup… Dinners are a great way to get motivate large gifts. Forget cake … let them eat steak.**
**— Robert G. Lee**

Set up your dinner for success by removing everything from the presentation portion that will distract from what you are doing. That would include a pre-set time when the servers are leaving the room so you can speak without interruption. Yes, it does make a difference.

Do this with your private presentations in restaurants, also. Prepare the wait staff ahead of time. When they see that you have your notebook out, they are to stay away from the table. If you explain that their tip will be determined by their ability to listen to that rule, they will understand. When I'm presenting to a small group at a restaurant, I always prep the manager and the waiter. Sometimes I have to excuse myself during the dinner and call the waiter over personally to give him the game plan. Do this and win. You are paying the bill. They work for you. Don't let a waiter lose you thousands of dollars because you're too embarrassed to take authority and tell them what you want. You're in the leadership chair, be that leader.

We certainly can't deliver captivating stories while trying to butter rolls, dress our salads, or ask for more butter. Use the dinnertime to talk about the wonderful people who are part of your organization. Stories of volunteers who are serving you. Share the names of other influential people who support you. The wealthy are affected by peer pressure too. Save your captivating pitch until you're ready to ask for the money. Don't drag it out too long. Eat dessert quickly, then go into your story and your ask.

I have seen concert situations deliver decent money and deliver a lot of new people to cultivate for a future dinner-style presentation. If you are presenting your work at a concert, continue to prevention method. Keep it short, keep it positive, keep it motivational, don't forget to actually ask for money. Have a way to receive it right then and there.

Use concerts to collect names that will then be moved to a dinner situation for further financial development.

## TAKEAWAY:

Food is a wonderful friction reducer for the wallet and checkbook. Better donors need better food. Whether behind a podium or a dinner plate, present with passion. Draw them into a captivating story, not into services and tasks. Your presentation needs to be swift and uninterrupted. During one-to-one dinners, you can talk about their family and the joy of your work, but when it comes to the closing, go back and deliver your SIX-Rs with passion.

# 16

## More 55-Second Presentations

**Whatever you do, work at it with all your heart, as working for the Lord, not for human masters.
— Apostle Paul**

The Carter administration brought us the 55 mph speed limit in an effort to conserve on fuel. I believe it was the band Van Halen that took him to task with a platinum album proclaiming they could not drive fifty-five. At my age, I know that fifty-five is the magic number for full acceptance into the AARP Club. Don't laugh, next year I get ten percent off at Bob Evans. I find that fifty-five minutes is a long time when you're trying to keep people laughing at a rate of seven laughs per minute—the average laugh count for a professional—and even fifty-five seconds can be a long time for a listener if you fill those seconds with boredom.

Many fundraisers struggle to achieve the needed presentation time on someone else's program. Approach the average pastor and ask to speak to his people, and he will tell you there is little time in his service for you. Let's be honest, his people will only give the church about one hour a week. If you are going to get on his platform, you may have to promise him a fifty-five second presentation and learn to actually deliver it. We already know it can be done. Advertisers do it with less time between every segment of your favorite episode of Little House on the Prairie, and so can you.

The same SIX-R presentation that will bring you success in fundraising will work for other presentations, although you may not use all the R's in every presentation.

The same SIX-R presentation should also be used for your video presentations. The slow death that is delivered by most video presentations could make John Logie Baird sorry he invented the video camera.

- Do you have a 55-second "Baby Bottle Boomerang" speech?
- Do you have a 55-second "Post-Abortive Bible Study" speech?
- Do you have a 55-second "Walk Information" speech?
- Do you have a 55-second "Volunteer Honor" speech?

You need every one of those. You might be thinking that these speeches don't ask for money. The SIX-R principles work for any talk that is asking for a response, whether it be for money, volunteers, or even prayer. For the record, as a leader, your every speech is part of a preparation for a future financial ask.

Below, you will find what I believe is the best way for you to get in front of a church audience. Honor your own volunteers. Every one of your volunteers go to a church somewhere, and many of those churches have never let you speak in front of them. Contact the pastor and explain that you want forty-five seconds to honor a member of their church with a plaque. All of the other volunteers are getting honored this way at their church. This is called peer pressure. Explain that you will provide him with a forty-five-second script before you speak, and if he preferred, he could actually read it and do the presentation (this is even better).

## SAMPLE 45-SECOND VOLUNTEER SPEECH

"Hello, my name is Deborah Best and I am the director of the Loving Arms Pregnancy Center. Right now, I'm going to honor a life-saver. Marjorie Smith, please stand. For the past year, Marjorie has been volunteering at the Loving Arms Pregnancy Center and has helped save sixty-four babies from abortion and helped hundreds of mothers along the way. I have a wonderful plaque of appreciation to give her today. Please stop by the Loving Arms Pregnancy Center table in the foyer at the end of the service and personally tell Marjorie how proud of her you are as well."

The well-prepared fundraiser has a photo to show on the video screens the entire time you, or the pastor, are reading this. The photo shows Marjorie standing in front of your Loving Arms sign. Never underestimate the power of the subliminal photo message. Set up a table and pass out cards to everyone who talks to Marjorie after the service.

Of course, this speech didn't ask for money. This speech is designed to get people interested enough to talk to you at the back of the room. That is when you get to deliver another 90-second presentation. That presentation includes the ask to come and visit or to attend a volunteer training. If you don't do this in the churches of every one of your volunteers every year, you are missing a wonderful opportunity.

## TAKEAWAY:

Use the SIX-R fundraising presentation outline in any presentation that you make. Never talk unless you have something captivating and motivational to say.

Say that message clearly, swiftly, and include some type of call to action.

# 17

## Find Your Free Money

### The wise man prepares for the next generation. — Solomon

How would you like to have an extra one hundred thousand dollars this year? It's in the bank. Go withdraw it. Use it where you need it. What do you mean it isn't there? What happened? Who robbed you? Call the police. Who should we arrest? Maybe we should arrest your organization's board from twenty years ago. Let's briefly gain an understanding of long-range funding and remind your board not to rob money they should be preparing for your organization to use twenty years from now. The major responsibility of any board is to secure funding for the future of an organization. Most board members put their name to an official document on that promise.

The word endowment is a wonderfully wealthy sounding word. It goes right along with charitable trusts in my dictionary of favorite words to hear. You see these terms in the closing credits of every PBS documentary. We all could name a few well-known names who appear on those lists of generous people.

This book isn't large enough for me to explain how to chase and obtain large endowment money, but let me get you up to speed so you won't be ignorant. As your organization grows to the place where your board believes that you will be here for a length of time, you will want to start preparing to be here for an extended length of time. Your board may wish to convince your donors to become long-term donors through their wills and trusts. Have you done that yet?

This is why you hear large organizations offer to supply free professional counseling on estate planning, wills, and trusts. This is their way of talking to people about how they will leave a lasting financial legacy. In fact, one might say that those who truly believe in the work of your organization should include your organization in their will. This would include every board member. We should support that which we believe in. Unfortunately, the poor fundraising practices of many organizations deliver no future for future generations.

Let me give you one of many possible ways a person might give charitably in an estate trust. A donor like yourself might choose to give your house through a charitable trust agreement to your favorite charitable organization with the legally predetermined arrangement that you can reside in the home until your death. Now, in most states, that property goes into the name of the non-profit trust organization and is kept by the organization until your death. What is the advantage? Taxes. If your property is owned by a non-profit, you aren't paying taxes on it anymore, plus the tax deduction makes for a very-large gift. There is a reason why wealthy people use these tax tools. This gives you a yearly tax break and cash in your hand now. It keeps your family from fighting over money, as your assets are already spoken for in advance of your passing. The donor knows that their most beloved charity is secure in the future. This principle can be great for anyone who owns a home or valuable property.

This book is not the place to give you a full understanding of all the options. Think of this chapter as a teaser. Assign a board member to search for more information. Interview organizations who are doing this well. Why can't you be one of them?

## TAKEAWAY:

Every wise Christian organization uses estate planning to their advantage. It would behoove you to find a professional service to prepare your organization for the future. Be wise and live for the next generation.

# 18

## Eve … and Adam

**Awaken the mighty men.**
**— Prophet Joel**

There is something I know without a doubt. For the past decade, I have had the joy of raising millions of dollars for well-deserving organizations. I have helped hundreds of organizations to double and triple their previous best banquet gifts simply by understanding how to make a very good financial ask and lubricating wallets with laughter before that serious presentation. My track record has proved that laughing people give more than crying people. However, there is another reason for my personal success. It's understanding that men are the gateway to larger gifts. You have to connect with the men. In both your private presentations and your large group presentations, if Adam isn't there, Eve will most often not feel empowered to give you a large gift. You need both the husband and the wife to be involved in your presentations. You must speak in a style and fashion that men can assimilate in their male minds. This is one reason why we want to do our presentations in such a concentrated manner—men can't (or won't) remain focused for long time lengths.

**When I need to know that my husband has heard and understood me, I know that I better present my case in one very clear sentence. Then I have him repeat it back to me at least twice. Then I will most likely text him later, just to make sure.**
**— Terica Williams**

Eve … and Adam Axiom: One table seated with eight women will deliver you, on average, $700. The same table with four men and their wives will deliver you, on average, $2,500.

Why is that? Do men care more? No. Most women, although not all, do not feel comfortable giving gifts over one hundred dollars or committing the family to monthly gifts unless their husbands are in agreement. I know there are exceptions. I also know those big gifts from "financially liberated" women can be even larger if their husband is present. Make sure that you are making your fundraising presentations to both the husband and the wife. You want to close that ask with the ability to receive the check. Hearing "Let me try to articulate all of this to my husband later this week" is most often going to be a financial failure. You may get a gift, but having the spouse hear the presentation will result in their joint approval of a greater gift.

When I plan my presentations, I speak to the men. I already know the women are on board with the PRC agenda. Men are bottom-line guys. Tell them what it takes to solve the problem, get their checks, and let them get back to the grueling work of watching football or playing golf. If you cannot learn to speak to men with authority and clarity, find a fundraising person among your board who can.

**The male mind must have its thought pods carried from one point to another by wild squirrels. We zig-zag over to there. Freeze! Wait … now we zig-zag over there. Whoops! I lost the pod. What time is it? Do you have any peanuts?**
**— Terica Williams**

Where have you chosen to make your small group or one-to-one presentation? Does it have televisions on the wall? Don't go there. Men are easily distracted. You have to have them in a place where they aren't distracted by passing cars or passing people. In a small presentation, select seating that puts your listener facing the wall, not the door or window. Does the restaurant you're using have a special room for parties? Would that restaurant let you use that room when you are doing repeated private fundraising dinners with multiple donors over the course of the year? I will bet they would if you give them all of your business. I'll bet they would set up an account so the check never came to the table. Bonus.

Make your large group presentations (banquet or gala) male friendly. Have something to specifically draw men. If possible, in larger group presentations, have a male asking for the money. Men take encouragement best from other men who are giving male peer pressure. Have testimonies from other men who give to your organization. Serve the food quickly. In some demographics, you may find the male donor base doesn't like to dress formally. Men hate long lines. Email and text everyone their table number before the event. Have signs in the parking lot and every forty feet from there to your event. Men hate to appear as if they don't know where they're going. Your signage can help them feel like the human GPS they want their wife to believe they are. Then, with all that in place, you can know that a happy man is a giving man.

Many group presentations are including a putting challenge before the event where the man could win a set of new putters. Many centers give every man who attends five tickets for the shotgun or Bass Pro Shop gift card giveaway that's going to be drawn at the end of the night. What have you done to help your ladies bring their men? As the chief fundraiser, you need to take charge of the dynamics going on before, during, and after your event.

On a one-to-married couple presentation, what little gift basket have you brought to the table for them? Could you bring a box of handcrafted stationary to the women? Your volunteers can make this in the office in between client visits. You could bring the man a tire pressure gauge or a LED flashlight. A good book is great for both of them.

Recently, I wrote a donor-centric book to promote giving to your center entitled Thank You for Saving My Life. Please check it out at Amazon.com. It contains twenty stories of lives saved as a result of local PRCs, pregnancy homes, and adoption connections. Every chapter closes with a thank you to those who support the work locally. I can recommend this book without shame, as 100 percent of the profits go to support a third-world PRC. Order one and see why this book should be in your fundraising arsenal.

Does the book you are giving promote what you are doing or the work that another type of ministry is doing? If you give a donor a book about the great work of a political-based organization, that could tell your donor their money is best placed where you seem to be most impressed. This is the reason we wrote Thank You for Saving My Life.

## TAKEAWAY:

Without connecting to the male mind, you could be losing seventy-five percent or more of the possible donation amounts. You must find ways to connect with Eve and Adam together in all your presentations. Get creative.

# 19

## Finding Millennial Money

**Rejoice, O young man, in your youth, and let your
heart cheer you in the days of your youth. Walk in
the ways of your heart and the sight of your eyes.
But know that for all these things
God will bring you into judgment.
— King Solomon**

Born between 1977 and 1995, and numbering almost
eighty million, Millennials (Gen-Y and Echo Boomers)
have grown up having the latest greatest stuff pitched
to them by the best of the advertising world. Since
they were toddlers growing up in front of the big
screen, their larger-than-life visuals were designed to
stimulate a desired effect. That effect was to

convince them to convince their parent(s) that total happiness and peace in the home would come from the purchase of a certain name-brand toy. The Millennial mind understands good marketing. They even appreciate it. They are the most culturally enfolded, politically diverse group that mankind has seen. This casserole of diversity is making new rules for the marketing professional every day.

This generation comes from a different history book. This Millennial generation will not remember a time when abortion was not the norm. Prayer was never in their schools. Evolution was taught to them as fact, not as theory. They will not personally remember Roe V. Wade, and some may not remember the September 11, 2001 Trade Center attacks. Those events will always have been in their history books and represented only by small, one-sided documentaries on public broadcasting channels. Depending on your age, you may have a real hard time thinking like this generation.

**It took a few decades for the seed of John Lennon and the Beatles to grow to fruition.**

**Imagine there's no heaven, no hell, no religion. We sang it long enough, for a new generation it has become a discouraging reality.**
**— Terica Williams**

When speaking to this generation, you must use illustrations they can generationally relate to. I realized this a few weeks ago, when I was telling a story about my desire to develop an app that would allow me to install Dr. Billy Graham's voice on a GPS. I imitated his traditional vocal style, saying, "Go two blocks and turn right on the narrow road. Not the broad way. The broad way leads to destruction. If you're on that road, make a U-turn immediately." I produced that sentence in a mirror perfect, dead-on vocal impersonation of Dr. Billy Graham. Then I realized that my young audience didn't know who Dr. Billy Graham was, nor did they care.

**Let no one despise you for your youth, but set the believers an example in speech, in conduct, in love, in faith, in purity.**
**— Apostle Paul**

When it comes to raising money, the Millennial presentation SIX-R outline is the same. However, the illustrations and passion factor may come from different foundations.

Millennials see themselves as members of a global community. They are citizens of the whole world, not just the United States. This is a generation that has been brought up thinking about global impact, as well as local community impact. They are less connected to any biblical absolute, as their parents, priests, and pastors did not convincingly forward that DNA to them. There are social arguments (not biblical arguments) that must be won in the eyes of a Millennial for them to join your team. You must sell them on how saving children in a world that, as they have been taught, will not be able to feed our current population in ten years is the right thing to do. You will have to sell them on how we would pay for 1.5 million children who would unfortunately be added to the welfare rolls in each coming year if we actually did stop abortion. This is another reason why overturning Roe V. Wade should never be part of your presentation platform to a Millennial.

These are kids who grew up cheering as the Bill Gates Foundation offered a million-dollar bounty to anyone who could produce a natural-feeling condom to help control the overpopulation of the world. This generation has had sex, sexual activity, sexual perversion, and sexual misconduct forced into their mind their entire lifetime. Your abortion story is not going to shock them into emotional connectedness with you. This generation came up during a time when everybody, including the pastors and priests, had some secret sexual thing going on. There is nothing considered weird or kinky to this generation. Don't get angry. They are products of our trickle-down environment. It's our generation that shaped their minds. If there's someone to blame, it's us. Get over it and deal with what it is.

These Millennials watched the Abstinence Educational Movement fail to gain traction as these groups, in their religious beliefs, refused to talk about any type of sexual protection. At least in the Millennial mind, this stand took the conservatives off the reality playing field and gave them little or no impact in the public schools these Millennials would graduate from. This generation sees our mistakes, and like generations before them, they want to disassociate from them. Does your organization have any good answers for this generation? Is your organization delivering messages that do not work, or are you still trying to fight Roe V. Wade? Think about it for a minute. To this generation, that would be similar to going back to fight for a woman's right to vote. Right or wrong, it's already fought. Move on.

**You cannot shock this generation.**
**— Jack Eason**

Over-exposed is the word I think of when I see our younger generations. Anyone can become calloused to things they see every day. The Millennials and their children, who are yet to be stereotyped by a name, have seen everything. Their internet and SnapChat has delivered them the bold naked reality of the entire world, and it's done so in living color. They have seen so many tragedies, so many wars, so much nudity, so much sexual perversion, so many abortions, so much godlessness, and so many civic and Christian leaders debunked, they cannot be shocked anymore. What will be your captivating statement to engage this generation?

The key to presenting to this generation is the same donor need outline that we looked at earlier, yet the story that will draw them in will not be, "We can stop abortion," but rather, "We are able to save the life of this child and transform this family because of your participation." You are going to have to show complete transformation to prove your value to this generation. There will be no "Abortion Wrong - Life Good" narrative pre-installed on their cerebral lobes. Abortion may not be considered completely out of the question to this group—even the more fundamental ones—although they will support you in your efforts to serve the overall community. On a good note, this generation may be more apt to personally volunteer than any other generation.

**Be nice to the young people. They will decide which nursing home you go to.**
**— Mark Lowry**

This is the generation who is likely to sarcastically remind you where the Bible exonerates the killing of women and children of oppositional cultures to save their own Hebrew culture. This can be a brief distraction. They may show you where Jesus declared it would be better if this person were not born and use that as an argument for the acceptance of early-term abortion for those in horrible family situations. The internet will provide them with plenty of source material for them to discuss. You must drag them into a successful narrative where they can see and feel a picture of Jane and her boyfriend becoming a thriving family within the tragedy of an unwanted or unplanned pregnancy. The story must show how the child brings fulfillment, joy, and a hand out of poverty to their parents' lives. Your story must meet the felt need of the Millennials you are talking with. Your own felt need is both irrelevant and a modern to post-modern world away.

## TAKEAWAY:

Lead your Millennials into a success story without getting political. Your Millennial donors will include more Democrats and Independents than your current donor base does. Stay out of politics. This generation will not think it good to see the local Republican or Democratic senator at your banquet. This is a generation of compromise for the greater good, so demonstrate your part in the greater good. Don't offend, save lives. Decide what your message is. If your message is "Become an Anti-Abortion Pro-Life Republican," then prepare to be disappointed. Make your message, "Join us in rescuing the children who will hold the future answers to world problems." Make that your one and only message.

## A POSSIBLE MILLENIAL NARRATIVE:

"When you save a child, you save the world. Every little boy and girl is a precious, lovely pearl in the making. We are called to help them grow and teach them well so they can one day save the world. Help us save the child whose mind holds the cure to cancer, poverty, famine, injustice, racism, and can bring world peace. Help us save the next MLK, the next Ghandi, or the next Bono."

# 20

## Your Money Tree

**Hard work brings a profit,**
**but mere talk leads to poverty.**
**— King Solomon**

Scholars debate the effects of two Hebrew words found in part of the book of Genesis. The words bara, (ex nihilo in Latin) for "out of nothing," and asah, which is believed to mean "to make something out of the material you have at your own disposal." Many scholars declare that God made the heavens and the earth out of nothing, but everything else He made from pre-existing matter. Finally, my years in Old Testament Hebrew studies have paid off with a two-sentence paragraph opening. That was worth four years.

Unless you are God, you need something to make something else. You need a seed, a foundation, a wealthy generous aunt, or even a good endowment would be helpful. Let me put it this way: You need money to make money. Any businessman with any little tiny bit of business sense knows that. It's an axiom. It's biblical. You must start with a seed. Only God can incorporate the "bara" word and make something out of nothing, and scholars say He hasn't done that in a long, long time.

We're in a world that frowns on the word fundraising. They hate that the cost of fundraising is being taken from their gift. They love it when events can be sponsored in their entirety by a third party so their gift is going one hundred percent to the worthy cause. We see modern organizations like Charity Water and my own Cups of Cold Water mission accomplishing it. But how do we do that?

Wise boards create a separate development fund with its own bank account. They do this because they are wise businesspeople. These wise, business-smart board members, directors, and development directors make all of their personal donations to the development fund account. Now there is a pre-existing account from which the cost of fundraising can be taken. Now we can prove to our donors that one hundred percent of their gift is going to the mission statement and not to fundraising overhead or the chicken and cold green beans on their banquet plate. That, of course, includes your personal small group dining presentations. I love to tell a donor that one of our board members is paying for our dinner tonight. Often that board member is me, but I don't need to say it. This is an encouragement to a smart businessperson regarding your organization's business prowess. In the paraphrased words of the Apostle Paul, "Let us not be ignorant."

Do you have a development account set up? Why not? When will it be set up? When will your own wise board begin to fund it? This is very important in the grand scheme of asking for money. It is your ability to tell them that you are not spending their money on anything other than the mission. Do you see the importance of this?

## TAKEAWAY:

Set up a development account at your bank and fund it with the gifts from your inner circle of board members, staff, super donors who understand that it takes money to make money, and you. Use this account to fund all your fundraising efforts. Work with business wisdom. Unless you can get something out of nothing (bara), you need to join the rest of us who need seed money to start our money tree.

# 21

## One Effective, Annual Ask

**Ask and you will receive,
and your joy will be complete.
— Jesus Christ**

Unfortunately, your ministry is not always judged by the work you actually do. All too often your ministry is judged by your ability to get good food on the table quickly, make the video work properly, provide comfortable chairs, be exciting while not asking "too hard" for money, and do it all in the course of ninety minutes. You may also have to perform this culinary combination without board members helping you or even showing up. Welcome to the real world.

Almost every organization produces some type of larger-format annual stewardship or fundraising event. Those who don't should. I often hear, "But they require so many man hours to produce." Yes, but take a look at what you aren't receiving from a great fundraiser, and you can clearly see they are more efficient than nothing at all. "But we never do well at those events." Then you're doing the events wrong. You are not an enigma. You are not the only one in the world who has your type of people. History repeats itself—unless we do something to stop it from repeating. We must take responsibility to re-educate (develop) our audience.

If you've had me teach Simple PRC Board Success Training or heard me speak over the past decade at Care-Net, Focus on the Family, or Heartbeat seminars, workshops, or main stage presentations, you've heard me confess, with great angst, to a great problem. That problem is that people don't judge you by your ability to do good work all year long; they judge you by your ability to serve a good dinner and produce a great show one

night at year. This is not fair. But it is what is. Men—
who tend to be little more judgmental in production
areas—are especially critical. I've heard numerous
times, "If they can't operate a video projector, how
can they run a quarter-million-dollar business?"
We've all made blanket judgements this way at some
point in our life, so maybe this is, as the old song
said, just good-old-fashioned karma coming back
around.

Most wise organizations will do a yearly ask,
seeing they are by far the most successful way to
receive large sums of money from large groups.
Many wise organizations will have Friend-Raising
events (like LaughForLife.us) to gain a higher-quality
audience at those yearly stewardship events. The
truth is, you must do your stewardship events well.
There are no excuses. The BanquetMoney.com
website is a step-by-step guide to a financially
successful event. But you have to use it. You cannot
blame the audience for a poorly produced banquet.
Banquets work. If they aren't working for you, it's not
the fault of the audience.

Let's go back to the question I love so much: Why are we doing everything we're doing? When preparing a banquet, you start by asking the reason why you are doing the banquet. Why are you doing this banquet? To gain awareness? STOP. A banquet is a very inefficient way to achieve awareness. Don't throw banquet dollars away to gain awareness. To gain volunteers? STOP. A banquet is a very inefficient way to corral volunteers. Don't throw money away. To overturn Roe V. Wade? STOP. A banquet is a very inefficient and stupid way to bring about legislative change. You do a fundraising banquet to raise funds. Yes, but STOP again. A banquet is a very inefficient way to gain money unless you do the banquet correctly. I know you went to a training ten years ago—or last year. Well, that was last year's input, wasn't it? The reason I'm doing this book on CreateSpace is so that I can update the information every year. We learn things, so let's move forward. Just because we are Christians does not mean that we need to be twenty years behind the times, although one might think that from observance of our presentations.

**I can do all things through
Him who gives me strength.
— Apostle Paul**

A good banquet will bring in money. A great banquet will bring you monthly donors and wonderful individual gifts. A bad banquet will lose money, lose your credibility in the community, and discourage any volunteers from joining you. Don't fail. To succeed, you take everything you know about presenting an ask for money, and you weave it into a tapestry of one hundred minutes. Let me give you a quick check list.

Answer these questions about a person-to-person (small group) ask and bring the answers forward to your large group event:

1. Would you choose a restaurant that was extremely slow and the food was dry and miserable? No. However, I see it all the time at banquets where there is no performance

guarantee given by the caterer or hotel. Eat quickly and talk clearly.

2. Would you want your wait staff to continue to interrupt your presentation asking to refill your coffee? No. However, I see it all the time when event leaders do not prepare their room for their audience to be able to listen without distractions.

3. Would you bring in a guest singer for a few table side songs or lead twenty minutes of worship in the midst of your one-to-one financial presentation? Most likely not. However, I see it all the time at banquets where directors thought it would be a good thing because they didn't think to ask the why question.

4. Would you forget to have the ability to receive funds on the donors' terms? I hope not. However, I see it all the time at banquets where directors simply didn't prepare to take checks, electronic gifts, or credit cards. Be prepared for a victory.

5. Would you show numerous slide presentations that had nothing to do with your financial request or interrupt that one-to-one presentation to give

awards to politicians or other banquet attenders? No. However, I see it all the time at banquets where focused slide shows of people who work at the center are played for eight minutes. Does your husband like to look at other couples' office photos? That doesn't sound like fun for the men I know. Stay focused.

6.  Would you allow the restaurant to dictate your serving times? No. However, I see it all the time at banquets as caterers tell the clients what they're going to do and when. If the meal is being served, you choose to have the salads and dessert pre-set. You pay the bill, be the leader.

7.  Would you allow an unprepared board member and a local pastor to sit at your table and remind them that you will be asking them for money at the end of the dinner and share a quick devotional about abortion? No. However, I see this at banquets all the time. How many times should you do a financial ask? Once. And it should be done perfectly and only following your captivating presentation.

Set up your group stewardship events with the same thought and professionalism you bring to an individual ask situation. In fact, when you do create the intimacy and direct approach of a personal appeal at your group events, you will see your dollars per donor rise.

## TAKEAWAY:

Bring all your acquired asking knowledge into every aspect of your stewardship events. It will bring you increased donations through wise financial communications. What you do in small groups does translate to larger groups. Bring the power of minimal story while understanding the Seven Donor Needs continue to remain the same. The bigger the group, the more focused you have to be. Group presentations don't allow for retakes.

# 22

## Deserve Good Funding

**Let your light so shine before men, that they may see your good works and glorify your Father which is in heaven.**
**— Jesus Christ**

Don't build your legitimacy on the illegitimacy of another organization. We often spend so much time trying to tell people how bad those other groups are, we never perfect our own work. My wife Terica wrote another little Post-It note here, saying, "It is much easier to attack the success of others than it is to get people to support our own lack of success in fulfilling our own mission promise." Good point. And ouch.

**Instead of complaining about the current state of affairs, we need to offer better alternatives. We**

**need to stop cursing the darkness and start lighting some candles.**
**— Mark Batterson**

In past years, a few videos have surfaced showing a conversation between an alleged Planned Parenthood representative and a couple pretending to be body part buyers. PRCs all over the country tried to use that to motivate people to give to their organization. Great speakers had to shorten their polished fundraising presentations so the audience could sit through what they had seen on Fox News fifty times already that morning. Audiences were already desensitized. Why were they doing it? The video didn't shock me a bit, not even the first time I saw it. How could I, as a self-proclaimed intelligent person, think that a group that would abort a fetus only minutes before a natural birth would not sell the body parts for a profit? I am pro-life, not pro-naive. Wake up leadership. Use an illustration without beating it into the ground. This illustration was great the first ten times we saw it, then it became old news and made our cause look something other than fresh.

Christian or not, we are in an age of freshness. Don't be ten years ago. Don't be last week. Don't be yesterday. To the post-modern mind they are the same.

World renown theologian John R. W. Stott warned often of the loss of confidence in the message we proclaim. He believed that we were losing ground because we could not truly, in good conscience, teach with passion what we did not fully believe. I believe he was right, and his illustration works on multiple levels. If you don't believe that your organization is doing great work, fix that first. I have done board training with many PRCs across the country. During that training, I realized the board members themselves did not believe they were doing a good job, yet they continued to go forward with mediocrity. Their stats often proved that.

A businessman overviewing two different PRCs said, "These centers are not really trying to reach abortion-minded people. You can't have a picture of a mother holding a baby next to a Christian cross and a Jesus fish on your sign and think that abortion-minded women are going to flock through your doors thinking you might help them get an abortion. You are either business illiterate, thus not deserving of my financial support, or simply lying to your donors about your genuine mission statement."

Tom Ahern is one of the country's most sought-after creators of fundraising messages. You might want to familiarize yourself with his material. Tom has said, "If you call yourself Save the Whales, every once in a while you have to save a whale."

If I was to be quoted on this topic, I would prefer that you put it this way. Mike Williams says, "We have a God-given mandate to be an organization worth funding. We must be wise in our business practices, honorable in our accounting, and effective in fulfilling our stated mission, because beyond our donors, we will one day answer to a higher authority."

If we are going to deserve good funding, we need to be successful in our work on the client (non-donor) side of the table. Are you? Do you honestly believe the work your organization does is a good work and that it's done at a reasonable dollar value? I am often more discouraged by the lack of wisdom, lack of business prowess, and lack of quality of the religious organizations than I am with the unscrupulous tactics of the left. As a relatively successful businessman myself, am I wrong to feel that way? However, this is not a commentary on the parachurch, it is a manual on how to raise money, so I will leave the morality and ethics to you. We each have to stand before God for our own work.

The point is, you will never be able to genuinely, without waiver, convince your donors or partners of your viability if you aren't truly viable in your own heart and mind. Unless you are a poker face champion, it will show. Be the team you would want to support.

## TAKEAWAY:

Promote your legitimacy not by wrongness of others, but by what you are doing right. We all gripe about negative political ads doing nothing more than bashing the opposing politician, while we resort to the same tactics. Use your current success to drive your future success in financial requests. People want to join a winning team. Be the winning team. Now, go ask for some money.

# 23

## Let's Remember…

### When I call to remembrance…
### — Apostle Paul

Let's go through and review the simple steps for your transformation to the "Super-Fundraising Professional" of your organization.

1.  Be worthy of support. Fulfill your mission statement well. Know that the organization you represent is business-practice smart and operating at a God-worthy level.

2.  Pray faithfully. Ask God for wisdom in finding the right people. Ask God to bring you creativity in sharing the message. Begin your prayer (and

fasting) months before you begin your presentations. Have your entire board participate.

3. Make your list(s) of potential donors. List the people you believe could give you more. List your own family members who aren't giving to this good work. List new contact possibilities. List deacons and elders and the pastors they're connected with. The Christian Business directory is a good place to look. A shooter without a target is going to miss the mark.

4. Secure appointments with past and potential donors. Work to get both husband and wife present for the presentation so your ask may receive an instant response.

5. Thoroughly understand the Seven Needs every great donor has to have met to pleasurably embrace your mission in a financial way. Know these donor needs so well that your every sentence promotes trust in your organization.

6. Prepare your short presentation, making sure that you have rapidly and thoroughly covered the SIX-Rs of a great fundraising presentation.

- We share the **REASON** they need to partner with us while captivating their attention. We share stories that move their emotions to respond. We use local illustrations. We present a solution that is doable. We might give an example of a success story and maybe even a loss as a result of being underfunded.

- We explain how the need can be successfully met with our **RESPONSE.** We advocate for a simple solution that cost a specific amount of money. Example: A twenty-five-thousand-dollar gift would save one hundred children next year and continue to do that for the next ten years. A gift of two dollars a day will save the life of one child from an abortion-minded mother and transform the mother and father along the way.

- We share the effectiveness of our organization in achieving **RESULTS.** We offer testimonials of success stories and utilize peer pressure by including the names of others who financially support our work. Look for names the listener might recognize.

- We **REMIND** the donor how much we, together, share the unified vision to solve the problem. We generate honest commonality with the potential donor or current partner by assuring them that both of you desire to be pro-life in a tangible, genuinely life-saving way. We present a problem narrative that together we cannot sit idly by and watch it continue. We present a solution narrative that together we cannot leave unfunded.

- We make our **REQUEST** for a dollar amount based on what we feel the donor could supply. We are not afraid to shoot for the moon, but we will accept a smaller planet if necessary. We never give a presentation without looking our friends in the eye and asking them to be a financial part of the solution.

- We come to the table prepared to **RECEIVE** their gift in whatever way they need to fulfill their gift.

That would include a pre-stamped, pre-addressed envelope. That would include a way to take a credit card payment. Be creative.

7. After securing the gift (or promise of the gift), we will follow up with a phone call, a handwritten thank you note, and a thank you from another person in the organization. At least three forms of gratitude should be administered for any newly registered partner. You cannot over-thank a donor. Get busy.

8. Find ways to rapidly demonstrate how their gift is being used for the cause it was intended. Prepare to prove your pitch, and use pictures if possible.

9. Find ways to invite the new partner into the inner sanctum of the work. Make them an intrinsic partner and confidant of your ministry. Some donors might want to be considered for board positions. Be careful. Some donors will not be as generous when they see the inside of the office. Move forward in this area with care.

**Let me tell you a secret that has led to my goal.
My strength lies solely in my tenacity.
— Louis Pasteur**

## TAKEAWAY:

Take the same Seven Donor need fulfillment into any presentation. Anytime we are looking for a specific outcome, we design our presentation to meet the donor needs of the specific person who can financially fulfill that outcome. Think demographically. This is a wisdom-filled, duplicable system that works. As you couple your hard work with prayer, you bring in the God factor, and that factor makes what you do go over the top. Now, go get your money.

# FOR YOUR INFORMATION

**If any person lacks wisdom let them ask...**
**— St. James**

**Mike G. Williams is available to speak at your next fundraising event.** Let Mike share the work of your PRC or adoption organization through his own powerful rescue adoption story and the rescue adoption of his son. This properly designed testimony will move your donors to dynamically support your work. Mike's statistics are among the best in the business. Please contact Gloria Leyda at the Ambassador Agency (615.370.4700 ext. 235) to secure him for a future year. View his PRC speaking references at www.FocusOnTheBanquet.com.

**Simple Board Success Seminar** is a 4-hour course that is taught by Mike G. Williams or his associates to help your board fully comprehend their part in the successful day-to-day and fundraising operational needs of the PRC. If you feel your board may not be performing up to their potential, they need to experience this seminar. This is not your normal PRC organization Standards & Practices training. This will train your board to be the intelligent donor and client specialists they have been called to be. Equip your board to succeed in the wonderful obligation they have accepted. This seminar will be the most fun you have ever had encouraging and equipping your board for success. Please contact Gloria Leyda at the Ambassador Agency (615.370.4700 ext. 235) for more information about hosting a Simple Board Success Seminar for your organization.

**Financial Success Consulting is available for you**. Would you like to have Mike G. Williams consult for your next fundraising event? Mike helps a number of organizations as their event consultant. If you are interested in this, the cost is extremely affordable. Contact Gloria Leyda at the Ambassador Agency (615.370.4700 ext. 235).

**FREE BANQUET PLANNING SCHOOL is available to you at www.BanquetMoney.com.** This is your one-stop shop for no-cost "UP TO DATE" training for your banquet preparation team. You can receive free outlines, free response card samples, and free pre-written director speeches. If you're not using the BanquetMoney.com information, which is updated monthly, you are living in yesterday's banquet world. Don't deliver a floppy disc banquet in a Bluetooth world. You can be fresh wherever you are.

**The Heart Share Group**. If you need a game plan for finding and developing donors, successful advertising strategies, special fundraising events, or online and interactive training, please contact this great team. See www.TheHeartShareGroup.com for more information.

Made in the USA
Middletown, DE
20 May 2017

# Magical Creatures

*By Elizabeth Pepper and Barbara Stacy*   Mystic tradition grants pride of place to many members of the animal kingdom. Some share our life. Others live wild and free. Still others never lived at all, springing instead from the remarkable power of human imagination.

# Ancient Roman Holidays

*By Barbara Stacy*   The glory that was Rome awaits you in Barbara Stacy's classic presentation of a festive year in pagan times. Here are the gods and goddesses as the Romans conceived them, accompanied by the annual rites performed in their worship. Scholarly, light-hearted – a rare combination.

# Celtic Tree Magic

*By Elizabeth Pepper*   Robert Graves in *The White Goddess* writes of the significance of trees in the old Celtic lore. *Celtic Tree Magic* is an investigation of the sacred trees in the remarkable Beth-Luis-Nion alphabet; their role in folklore, poetry, and mysticism.

# Moon Lore

*By Elizabeth Pepper*   As both the largest and the brightest object in the night sky, and the only one to appear in phases, the Moon has been a rich source of myth for as long as there have been mythmakers.

# Magic Spells and Incantations

*By Elizabeth Pepper*   Words have magic power. Their sound, spoken or sung, has ever been a part of mystic ritual. From ancient Egypt to the present, those who practice the art of enchantment have drawn inspiration from a treasury of thoughts and themes passed down through the ages.

# Love Feasts

*By Christine Fox*   Creating meals to share with the one you love can be a sacred ceremony in itself. With the witch in mind, culinary adept Christine Fox offers magical menus and recipes for every month in the year.

# Random Recollections I, II, III, IV

*By Elizabeth Pepper*   Pages culled from the original (no longer available) issues of *The Witches' Almanac,* published annually throughout the 1970's, are now available in a series of tasteful booklets. A treasure for those who missed us the first time around; keepsakes for those who remember.

*Use the order form on overleaf, or order online at www.TheWitchesAlmanac.com*

# Order Form

Each timeless edition of *The Witches' Almanac* is unique.
Limited numbers of previous years' editions are available.

---

**Special offer** – *1993/94 Almanac through the 2005/06 Almanac*
Bundle of 13 back issues for only $75, with free shipping. (*$113.35 value*)

---

_____ **2007 - 2008   The Witches' Almanac @ $9.95** _____

_____ 2006 - 2007   The Witches' Almanac @ $8.95 _____

_____ 2005 - 2006   The Witches' Almanac @ $8.95 _____

_____ 2004 - 2005   The Witches' Almanac @ $8.95 _____

_____ 2003 - 2004   The Witches' Almanac @ $8.95 _____

_____ 2002 - 2003   The Witches' Almanac @ $7.95 _____

_____ 2001 - 2002   The Witches' Almanac @ $7.95 _____

_____ 2000 - 2001   The Witches' Almanac @ $7.95 _____

_____ 1999 - 2000   The Witches' Almanac @ $7.95 _____

_____ 1998 - 1999   The Witches' Almanac @ $6.95 _____

_____ 1997 - 1998   The Witches' Almanac @ $6.95 _____

_____ 1996 - 1997   The Witches' Almanac @ $6.95 _____

_____ 1995 - 1996   The Witches' Almanac @ $6.95 _____

_____ 1994 - 1995   The Witches' Almanac @ $5.95 _____

_____ 1993 - 1994   The Witches' Almanac @ $5.95 _____

_____Bundle of 13 back issues (*Free shipping*) @ $75.00 _____

____ Witches' All @ $13.95 _____

____ Random Recollection I @ $3.95 _____

____ Random Recollection II @ $3.95 _____

____ Random Recollection III @ $3.95 _____

____ Random Recollection IV @ $3.95 _____

*Subtotal*_____

*Shipping & handling*_____

(*One book: $3  Each additional book add $1*)

*7% sales tax (RI orders only)*_____

*Total*_____

Send a check or money order payable in U. S. funds or credit card details to:
The Witches' Almanac, Ltd.  PO Box 1292, Newport, RI  02840-9998
phone/fax: (401)847-3388    toll-free phone/fax: (888)897-3388
*Email: info@thewitchesalmanac.com    www.TheWitchesAlmanac.com*